A YEAR
at the
TABLE

By Joby Wells

First published in Great Britain in 2017 on behalf of:
Albert's Table, 49c Southend, Croydon, CR0 1BF
www.albertstable.co.uk

Published by:
RMC Media – www.rmcmedia.co.uk
6 Broadfield Court, Sheffield, S8 0XF
Tel: 0114 250 6300

Text and design © RMC Media, 2017
Photography © Tim Green (www.timgreenphotographer.co.uk), 2017

Author: Joby Wells with Adam Kay, Martin Edwards and Jo Davison
Design: Richard Abbey
Proof-reader: Christopher Brierley

Printed and bound in Malta by:
Gutenberg Press Ltd – www.gutenberg.com.mt
Gudja Road, Tarxien, Malta, GXQ 2902
Tel: 00356 2189 7037

A CIP catalogue record for this book is available from the British Library.

ISBN: 978-1-907998-29-4

Contents

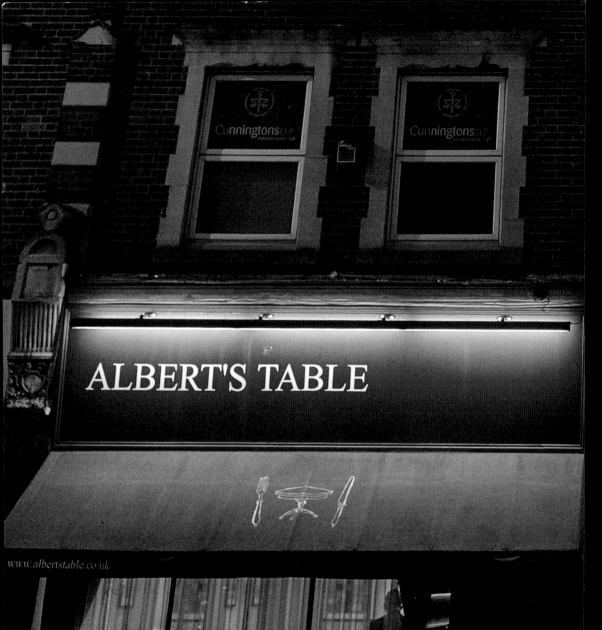

ALBERT'S TABLE

49b&c

020 8680 2010

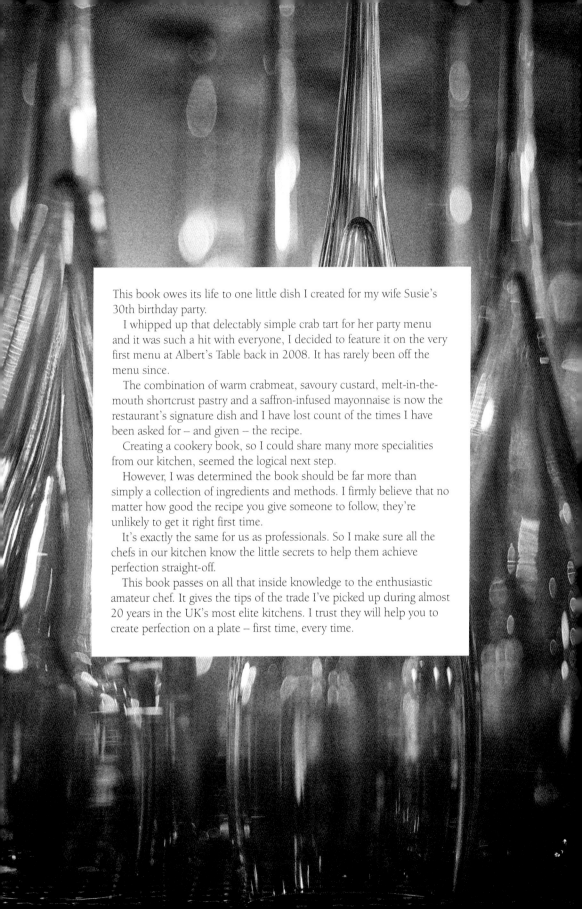

This book owes its life to one little dish I created for my wife Susie's 30th birthday party.

I whipped up that delectably simple crab tart for her party menu and it was such a hit with everyone, I decided to feature it on the very first menu at Albert's Table back in 2008. It has rarely been off the menu since.

The combination of warm crabmeat, savoury custard, melt-in-the-mouth shortcrust pastry and a saffron-infused mayonnaise is now the restaurant's signature dish and I have lost count of the times I have been asked for – and given – the recipe.

Creating a cookery book, so I could share many more specialities from our kitchen, seemed the logical next step.

However, I was determined the book should be far more than simply a collection of ingredients and methods. I firmly believe that no matter how good the recipe you give someone to follow, they're unlikely to get it right first time.

It's exactly the same for us as professionals. So I make sure all the chefs in our kitchen know the little secrets to help them achieve perfection straight-off.

This book passes on all that inside knowledge to the enthusiastic amateur chef. It gives the tips of the trade I've picked up during almost 20 years in the UK's most elite kitchens. I trust they will help you to create perfection on a plate – first time, every time.

Who is Albert?

It's the first question on every new customer's lips.
So, who IS Albert?

Many probably assume it's the name of our chef. Or some mystery VIP diner maybe. The truth is, the restaurant is named after my grandfather.

When it came to choosing a name for my own establishment, one that was the essence of the Great British food and values I was determined to focus on, and a passion for being the hospitable host, there was only one.

My grandad Albert adored the hearty, traditional dishes my grandma would make. He loved feeding people – the dining table was often crowded with family and friends.

I figured you don't get a more British figurehead than Albert. I wanted to get across that feeling that you were going to his house for dinner.

Albert lived in a little village outside Cambridge and was a greyhound breeder and trainer.

He grew his own vegetables and fruit and raised his own pigs. His generation was raised to be self-sufficient. That post-war generation had no choice but to grow their own vegetables. As a result, they lived off brilliant produce.

Even during World War Two, his family had plenty of food on their plates. In fact, his belly was so important to him that during the war years he bent the law a little bit to ensure this family never went without.

He would slaughter the pigs, butcher them himself and make his own bacon, swapping what he didn't need with food produced by other villagers; they had their own mini black market going on!

I think he would have loved to see his name above my restaurant door. Undoubtedly, he would have appreciated our food.

I reckon he would have approved, too, of the fact that I chose to base his restaurant in Croydon for the most sensible of reasons… That it was within cycling distance of home.

I've cycled to work for years and I wanted to continue. It's a really peaceful feeling at night, when you're cycling home from a shift in the pitch black and there's nobody else on the road. The 32-mile round-trip from Central London kitchens to my home in Kent was a bit much.

When planning where the restaurant should be, my wife and I drew a 10-mile radius around Kent on an ordnance survey map. Any new restaurant had to be inside the 10-mile line.

Now my trip is nine miles each way. Perfect. There's a massive hill behind the restaurant and at the end of the night, I sweat the mile and a half to the top. By the time I get to the brow, I've completely forgotten about work. Then it's downhill and flat all the way home.

The five seasons of food

I am a man for all seasons… All five of them.

I have an abiding passion for taking advantage of nature's abundant larder, and believe that when it comes to produce, there isn't only spring, summer, autumn and winter to reap from.

There is a glorious stretch which begins in early spring with eager shoots of asparagus, Jersey Royals and succulent young lamb and runs through to the bean and soft fruit gluts of late August; it simply cannot be classed as anything less than three seasons.

There is a vast amount of stunning food for us to work with during those five months. We keep our menus fluid so we can leap on whatever beautiful produce comes our way and inspires our cooking.

We have a secret weapon in getting the freshest of nature's table straight onto the plate at Albert's – a green-fingered local by the name of Grace Onions.

Grace has a passion for allotment growing and regularly arrives unannounced at our door with produce from her garden, which is just around the corner from us. A vat of Jerusalem artichokes, buckets of gooseberries, an armful of rhubarb… Every time she has a glut of produce, she shares it with us.

It's lovely to receive something you weren't expecting. You get your thinking cap on and make a feature of it. When Grace's produce is on the menu we proudly name-check her. Our regulars have got used to seeing her name next to dishes. In our quest to source locally, we simply couldn't get any more local than Grace's garden.

Joby's story

Were it not for a lucky break and the ability to chop a tomato, it's fair to say I would never have been a chef, let alone one who cut his teeth in some of the most lauded Michelin restaurants in London and now proprietor of my own establishment.

Albert's Table, which proudly bears a Michelin listing and two AA rosettes, has, I like to think, put Croydon on the culinary map.

As you've already read, the restaurant is named after my grandfather, Albert. As someone who loved his food, had his own allotment and adored entertaining, I like to think that he would have been incredibly proud of what I've achieved, if a bit surprised, considering that when he died I was an 18-year-old set on becoming an engineer.

He wasn't to know it, but the course of my life changed irrevocably the day I landed a pot-washing job in a restaurant kitchen during my year out before heading to university. I was expecting nothing more than a few months of hard graft and dishwasher hands. But opportunity fell into my lap.

On my first day, the guy doing the salads walked out. I said I'd step in – I thought it would be a laugh – and took off the Marigolds I'd literally just pulled on.

I never put them back on again. I did well enough to be given salad duties all summer long and found I really enjoyed the camaraderie of the professional kitchen, and although it was only salads, I genuinely enjoyed the new skills that I was learning.

When I eventually began my engineering degree, I discovered I didn't like it much. I missed the banter, the clatter and creativity of the kitchen and after my first year at university, took a year out to learn to cook. My engineering tutor thought I was joking when I told him.

On Tuesday afternoons I missed lectures to attend Nottingham catering college, though to be honest, being a chef still wasn't really my career choice. I just wanted to learn a skill that wasn't to do with engineering – and thought it would be a good idea to be able to cook decent food for myself.

I grew up in Cambridge, with good food on my plate. My family had a smallholding. There was usually a waddle of ducks under your feet, a cow, a couple of goats or a pig at my mother Judith's farm.

We always dined on vegetables from the garden. The pig and the cow would go for slaughter and return to mum's vast freezer in joints, chops, mince… You name it.

My mum is a great cook and utilised her skills to use every possible scrap. Nothing was wasted and everything tasted wonderful.

I thought that everyone did what my family did. Only when I moved away from home did I realise most people don't have a home-reared pig in the freezer or fresh eggs every day, but live on takeaways and ready meals instead of cooking. I didn't want to do that.

After graduating from university, I put my catering experience to use and landed a job as a commis chef at Hart's, a respected restaurant in Nottingham.

The head chef Mark Gough had worked in Two-Michelin Star restaurants in Lyon and the idea of that fascinated me. He had found the courage to head out there and bang on back doors at top restaurants, asking for a chance. I decided to follow his example… But instead of France, I headed to the Michelin Two-Stars in London.

I was 23 by then – most chefs start at 16, and had a good five years of experience on me. I wanted to accelerate my learning by working with the best of the best.

It was the wisest move I've ever made. I landed trial shifts at numerous elite establishments, but knew when I arrived at The Square in Mayfair that this was where I wanted to stay

It was one of London's most lauded restaurants – it only recently changed hands after 25 years. It was everything I'd imagined a great kitchen would be – everyone running around like crazy, and the food… It was stuff I'd never seen before. It couldn't have been any better.

I managed to impress chef-patron Phil Howard and his head chef Robert Weston enough to get taken on. I have to admit I nearly bottled it in my first week as commis on the pastry section. I remember asking my boss: "Have I bitten off more than I can chew here? I don't know anything!"

His reply was along the lines of: 'Push along and you'll be fine. If you don't want to push along, go and find another job.' It certainly wasn't a caring chat!

I'd already seen a couple of people come and go very swiftly and I really didn't want to be one of those people, so I did indeed push along.

The first few months were really tough. I was making so many mistakes I felt like an idiot. But I got my confidence and after that I never lost it. I moved on to new sections and made mistakes and cock-ups, but every time I told myself that after a couple more services I would be at the same level as everybody else.

Duck to water as a chef? I'm not sure about that. But prepared to push to get there? Definitely.

In 2004, having reached the level of Chef Tournant, I pushed on some more – and left to search for new challenges. I found them, but to be honest, with hindsight I do regret leaving The Square when I did. I am yet to find a kitchen that operates at such a pace, where the cooking was as superb and you weren't just a number, but respected and valued. That's rare in kitchens – really rare. It's what I strive for at Albert's Table.

The humble, honest cooking of acclaimed chef Bruce Poole drew me to my next job – at his Chiswick venue La Trompette. Showered with accolades since its launch, the restaurant had a reputation for serving some of the best food in London without the formality or prices associated with the capital's top end establishments.

I loved that the food ethos fitted entirely with the ones I had been raised on. I learned at the elbows of Britain's finest chefs, but I realised the most important principles of food as a child.

It was my family who taught me, by example, that the supreme taste and quality you get from food grown or raised with love, and so fresh it practically still squeaks, should be allowed to do its own talking. And home is where I bought into the eating of the whole animal.

At La Trompette chefs used their culinary skill to create stunning flavour from fish and cuts of meat that were less expensive than I had grown accustomed to at The Square – and they using everything, nose to tail. For me that felt the most natural way to cook.

I stayed two years and was the Senior Sous Chef of the team that earned La Trompette its first Michelin Star. That was a great feeling.

I would love to earn a Star at Albert's Table. We made the AA guide and received a listing in the Michelin Guide in 2016; we've got a bit of work to do yet, but a Star is definitely in our sights.

Respect for quality ingredients and the seasons that produce such vast and varied glory is at the very heart of Albert's Table. I strive to create food which doesn't merely nod at simplicity and the integrity of ingredients, but champions it.

I insist on produce which has been farmed with care and respect – we source our meat from good breeds that are fed well; we seek out vegetables that have been nurtured rather than forced and buy our fish and shellfish from sustainable sources.

It has taken years to find the right producers, but, it's been worth the effort. Great quality ingredients make our jobs easier – they are a dream to cook with.

The rump steak from our beef supplier is so tender and flavoursome we don't ever serve fillet. Customers say: 'What did you do to that piece of chicken?' The truth is we didn't do anything other than cook it nicely. The farmer ensured that the chicken tasted as good as it did.

I believe in letting that quality shine by keeping our dishes simple and clean. If a customer orders beef, then beef will be the star of the show. There will be a small, supporting cast on that plate, but it's there not to impress, but to bring out the best in the meat's flavour.

And the want-not, waste-not, years of my childhood have never been forgotten. Using everything up is an important part of a chef's learning; in fact many classical dishes are actually derived from peasant food, in which every scrap would be utilised.

I firmly believe that if an animal died for us to eat it, we should respect that, not waste it.

This book explains how we do things at Albert's Table. I have not changed anything or converted any methods for the home cook. This book is meant as a guide to how we do things and I hope that you take as you want from each dish that works for you.

We measure liquid in grams (g) a lot of the time, not in a measuring jug. It is nearly impossible to measure 5ml of liquid in a jug but easy to weigh 5g on the balance. 1g is about 1ml.

At home I would never 'dress a plate' I much prefer to 'family serve' where everyone can tuck in and help themselves. My advice would be that any recipes (especially the main courses) that look a bit tricky to dress – don't. It is more important to have everything cooked correctly and hot than to have it looking perfect on a plate and cold. Remember that at the restaurant we have four people dressing each plate – you will probably be on your own!

If you want to add some theatre to a special meal, rather than 'dress on', bring a big carving board and knife to the table and carve in front of your guests. Men especially enjoy getting involved in this.

All oven temperatures quoted in this book are electric fan unless otherwise stated.

Anyone that dines at Albert's Table will know that we have two menus – Destination and Market. I have included examples from both.

We cook all the fish with skin on, unless otherwise stated. I lightly score across the fish about 1mm deep about 5mm apart (you will need a very sharp knife for this). When cooking I always start in a warm pan with about 5mm of fat. Both of these methods will help prevent the fish from curling up and will give you an even crisp skin. Always cook the skin in oil and finish with butter at the end – this will prevent the butter from burning.

March April

Brandade croquette with rocket pesto, leaves & roasted garlic mayonnaise

Cornish lobster soufflé with samphire, brown shrimps & bisque sauce

Freshwater crayfish cocktail with horseradish, apple & cucumber

Slow-roast shoulder of Old Spot pork, with pearl barley, butternut & marjoram, prunes and apple sauce

Atlantic cod with chargrilled potato, deep-fried squid, celery & bisque sauce

Pan-fried brill with potato gnocchi, Norfolk mussels, carrot & ginger stew and fresh coriander

Rump of dry-aged Hereford beef, with little cottage pie, chargrilled leeks, celeriac & red wine

Grilled leg of Colne Valley hogget with crushed new potatoes, rainbow chard, olives & mint

Rhubarb pavlova with pistachio

Carrot cake with white chocolate mousse & poppy seed allumette

Brandade croquette with rocket pesto, leaves & roasted garlic mayonnaise

Brandade is a classic example of peasant food coming good. Back in the day, before fridges, fish would be salted to preserve it. Salt cod has many uses in the kitchen, but my favourite is brandade. By gently poaching salt cod in garlic infused milk, and then binding it with mashed potato and olive oil, you get a wonderfully rich creamy fishcake mix.

When garlic is roasted, it loses all of its bitterness and takes on a beautiful sweetness. In the restaurant, we make big batches of roasted garlic (see Basic Recipes) and then use it throughout the service instead of raw garlic.

Serves: 4

For the brandade croquettes:
400g Salt cod
Milk
Thyme
Bay
2 Garlic cloves
200g Mashed potato
(see Basic Recipes)
Olive oil
100g Flour
3 Eggs (beaten)
100g Panko breadcrumbs

1. Soak the salt cod in cold water for 6 hours – this will wash out the saltiness.

2. Place the cod in a pan and cover with enough milk to just cover the fish. Add some thyme, bay, and a couple of smashed garlic cloves. Cook the fish on a medium heat until it just simmers, and then remove. Allow the fish to cool in the milk.

3. Remove the cod from the milk and transfer it to a food processor. Add the mashed potato (it must be hot) and blend the two together. Add a good lug of olive oil and some of the poaching milk – you should have a stiff, well-flavoured mix.

4. Allow to chill and set in the fridge for a couple of hours. When firm and cold, take 40g portions and mould in your hands to little barrels. Roll each barrel in flour, then beaten eggs, and finally breadcrumbs. The croquettes are now ready to deep fry.

For the rocket pesto:
70g Rocket leaves, plus a few extra leaves to dress the plates
70g Roasted pine nuts
1 Garlic clove
140g Olive oil
70g Old Winchester Cheese, grated finely
Salt and pepper, to season

1. In a food processor, blend the rocket leaves, pine nuts, garlic and olive oil. When smooth, add the cheese and adjust the seasoning as required.

For the roasted garlic mayonnaise:

3 Egg yolks
100g Dry mash (see Basic Recipes)
50g Roasted garlic pulp (see Basic Recipes)
25g Lemon juice
225g Olive oil
175g Vegetable oil
Pinch of sugar
Salt and pepper, to season

1. In a food processor, blend the yolks, mash, garlic and lemon juice.

2. Mix the two oils and the sugar. In a gentle stream, pour the oil into the spinning food processor. When thick and glossy, season to taste.

3. Transfer to a squeeze bottle.

To serve:

1. Deep-fry the croquettes until they are golden brown and hot all the way through.

2. Dot the mayonnaise on to four plates – don't be shy, you want a bit of mayonnaise with each mouthful of brandade.

3. Drizzle the pesto on the plates and add a few rocket leaves dressed in a little olive oil.

4. Drain the croquettes on kitchen paper and then arrange in the middle of the plates. Serve with lemon wedges if desired.

Cornish lobster soufflé with samphire, brown shrimps & bisque sauce

Twice baking takes all the pressure off serving a soufflé, as you can have it ready to go in advance. Samphire is a sea grass; it can be stalky at one end, so do pick off the hard, woody bits.

Serves: 6

For the lobster stock:

3 Lobsters (approx. 450g each)
150g Butter
1 tbsp Tomato purée
100g Brandy
Water
Zest from 1 orange

1. Put the live lobsters in the freezer for 15 minutes. The cold will send them to sleep so that they don't feel anything when you cook them.

2. Drop the lobsters into a large pan of boiling water, cook for 5 minutes. After cooking, drop them into iced water to chill them – this will also arrest the cooking process.

3. Separate the lobsters into the shells and the claw and tail meat. Reserve the meat for later – you should have about 450g.

4. Smash the lobster bones with a rolling pin. In a wide shallow roasting dish, roast the bones in foaming butter. Add the tomato purée and cook out for 5 minutes. Add the brandy and reduce by half. Add just enough water to only just cover the bones and cook out for 25 minutes. Add the orange zest.

5. Remove from the heat and allow the flavours to mingle for 25 minutes. Pass through a colander allowing all the liquid to drip through, and then through a fine sieve. Chill the stock for later use.

For the soufflé base:

50g Pudding rice
110g Whipping cream
340g Lobster stock
50g Butter
Pinch of cayenne pepper
Seasoning

1. Pre-heat the oven to 120°C.

2. In an ovenproof pan, bring the rice, cream and stock to the boil, stirring as you go. Put a lid on the pan and transfer it to the oven. Add the butter and cayenne and cook out for 30 minutes (or until the rice is completely soft). Season to taste and remove from the heat.

3. Blend in a liquidiser and chill in the fridge.

For the soufflé:

Soufflé base (as above)
4 Egg yolks
130g Red Leicester cheese, grated
450g Chopped lobster meat
8 Egg whites
1g Table salt

1. Pre-heat the oven to 175°C.

2. Line six meticulously dry large pudding bowls with soft butter. Dredge with gram flour and then tap out any excess.

3. Warm the soufflé base in a bowl set over simmering water. Add the yolks and the cheese and beat for 2 minutes until it starts to thicken. Add the cooked lobster, remove the bowl from the heat.

4. Whisk the whites and salt in an electric mixer. Incorporate the whites into the lobster mix in batches of a third at a time until all the egg white has been incorporated. Spoon the mix into the lined moulds.

5. Place a roasting dish in the oven and half fill with boiling water. Place the soufflé moulds in the roasting tray and cook for 7 minutes.

6. Remove from the oven and allow to cool for at least 10 minutes. Gently tip the soufflé from the mould on to buttered greaseproof paper. Refrigerate.

Other ingredients:

500g Bisque sauce (see Basic Recipes)
100g Brown shrimps
100g Samphire (wash well)

1. Pre-heat the oven to 175°C with a roasting tray in it.

2. Slide the soufflés on to the hot tray and cook for 7 minutes.

3. Reheat the brandy sauce (lobster stock) in a saucepan. When it comes to the boil, remove from the heat and add the shrimps and the samphire. The heat of the sauce will warm the shrimps without overcooking them and wilt the samphire.

4. After 7 minutes, the soufflés will be well risen and golden. Slide them into warm bowls and ladle the hot sauce, samphire and shrimps over the top. Serve immediately.

Freshwater crayfish cocktail with horseradish, apple & cucumber

Crayfish are in abundance in British rivers. This dish is a take on the classic prawn cocktail and can be prepared in advance and assembled at the last moment. As with most things at the restaurant, we make sure we use every part of the crayfish; as well as the sweet tail meat, we make a bisque with the body shells.

Serves: 6

For the bisque dressing:
Bisque sauce (see Basic Recipes)
Olive oil
Zest of 1 orange
Lemon juice

1. Follow the bisque recipe, but using the crayfish shells.

2. When it is made, reduce it right down on a medium heat until it reaches the consistency of tomato soup. At this point it will taste very strong. Remove from the heat.

3. To three parts olive oil and one part bisque, add the orange zest and a few drops of lemon juice. You should now have a very fresh tasting bisque dressing. Pour into a squeeze bottle and allow to cool in the fridge.

For the crayfish cocktail:
2 Apples
½ Cucumber
2 Gem lettuce
1 Avocado
10 Crayfish tails
2 tbsp Crème frâiche
Salt and pepper, to season
Lemon juice

1. Peel the apples, remove the core and cut into four.

2. Peel the cucumber, cut in half and remove the seeds by running a spoon down the middle.

3. Cut the lettuce, avocado and crayfish into 5mm dice and bind with the crème frâiche so that it just holds. Season with salt, pepper and lemon juice. Put into a container with clingfilm over and refrigerate. This recipe only lasts one day as the avocado will start to discolour.

Other ingredients:
36 Crayfish tails
Bisque dressing
Chives
Cucumber
Celery salt
Coriander cress, to garnish

1. For each person allow 6 crayfish tails. Marinate them in the bisque dressing and some freshly snipped chives.

2. For each person, slice three pieces of cucumber 3mm thick and season with celery salt. Leave for 5 minutes and then pat dry with kitchen towel. Using a 2.5cm cutter, cut the disks of cucumber into neat circles.

To serve:

1. On each plate, place three slices of cucumber.

2. Using two spoons make a nice quenelle of the cocktail mix and place on top of each cucumber slice. Put two crayfish on top of each quenelle.

3. Finish the plate with a drizzle of the dressing and some fresh coriander cress.

Slow-roast shoulder of Old Spot pork, with pearl barley, butternut & marjoram, prunes and apple sauce

Whole shoulder of pork can be quite a large inconsistent joint. For individual portions we use the collar, which is the central joint that runs through the shoulder. It is a lovely, fatty, well-marbled piece of meat that slow cooks very well. A whole collar is about 2kg, so is perfect for about eight people.

Serves: 8

For the pork:
1 Pork collar
Salt
English mustard
10g Fennel seeds
10g Coriander seeds

1. The pork can be prepared the day before you want to eat.

2. Pre-heat the oven to 180°C.

3. Season the pork all over and leave at room temperature for 20 minutes to let the salt penetrate the meat. With a kitchen towel, pat the meat dry.

4. Pour the English mustard into a pot and then with a pastry brush, brush the pork liberally all over. Now roll the pork in the fennel and coriander seeds.

5. Place the pork onto an oven rack over a roasting dish. Quarter fill the bottom of the dish with water. Slide the pork into the oven and cook for about 30 minutes or until the pork starts to caramelise. At this point check that the water has not evaporated – if it has, add some more and then loosely cover the meat with kitchen foil. Turn the oven down to 120°C and carry on cooking until a knife or skewer can pass through the meat with very little resistance. This will take between 2 and 4 hours depending on your oven. Allow the meat to cool and then refrigerate overnight.

For the pearl barley butternut & marjoram:
300g Chicken stock
300g Pearl barley
2 Butternut squash
½ Bunch marjoram

1. Bring the chicken stock to the boil and season it to taste. Add the barley, bring back to the simmer, and cook out for about 20 minutes or until the barley is cooked, but still has a little bite. Remove from the heat and allow to cool in the stock.

2. Peel the butternut squash, cut in half and remove the seeds. Cut the squash into 5mm dice. Pick the marjoram from the stalks.

For the apple purée:
1kg Cox apples
100g Water
½ Lime

1. Peel, core, and roughly dice the apples.

2. In a heavy-based pan, add the apple and the water. With a lid on, cook out until the apples are soft. If the mix is still wet, remove the lid and cook out until a thick consistency is achieved. Blend the apple in a liquidiser until smooth. Squeeze in the lime juice and check the seasoning. Keep warm until ready to dish up.

Other ingredients:
50g Pumpkin seeds, toasted
5g Extra virgin olive oil
500g Madeira sauce (see
Basic Recipes)
18 Chopped prunes

1. Carve the pork collar into eight equal steaks and reheat under a grill. Turn every few minutes so that they heat evenly.

2. Whilst the pork is heating, pass the liquid from the barley into a clean pan and bring to the boil. Add the butternut dice and cook until tender. Add the barley to bring it back to temperature again, and then drain the whole lot through a colander. Stir in the toasted pumpkin seeds and chopped marjoram.

To serve:

1. With a spoon, swipe the apple purée around one side of the plate. Place a neat pile of the barley mix in the middle of the plate, and then finish with the pork.

2. Stir a little olive oil into the Madeira sauce and then spoon the sauce and the prunes over the pork and around the plate.

Atlantic cod with chargrilled potato, deep-fried squid, celery & bisque sauce

Early spring brings fabulous young celery. Don't confuse this with the stuff in the supermarkets; young celery is much smaller and has delicate leaves at the top of the shoots, it is more yellow than green. There is not a lot of preparation to this dish, but there is a fair bit to do last minute.

Serves: 4

2 Squid
100g Plain flour
Salt and pepper, to season
8 Young celery stalks
200g Chicken stock
1 Garlic clove
4 Sprigs thyme
1 Onion, sliced
4 x Cod fillet portions (150g each)
Chargrilled potatoes (see Basic Recipes)
Bisque sauce (see Basic Recipes)
Chervil, to garnish

1. Wash the squid, discard the beak and slice the body into 5mm rings. Cut the tentacles in half.

2. Season the flour with salt and freshly ground black pepper and then dredge the squid in the flour.

3. Cut the root from the celery and wash thoroughly in cold water.

4. Pre-heat the oven to 160°C.

5 Bring the chicken stock, garlic, thyme and sliced onion to the boil. Adjust the seasoning – it is important to have a well-seasoned stock. Gently poach the celery in the stock until it is just cooked.

6. In a heavy-based pan, fry the cod on the skin side until golden and crisp. Loosely cover in foil and transfer to the oven. Cook for about 5 minutes.

7. While the fish is cooking, chargrill the potato slices and keep warm.

8. Warm the bisque sauce.

9. Shake excess flour from the squid, and deep fry (170°C).

To serve:

1. Lay three celery stalks along the centre of each plate (you may need to trim them down if they are a bit long).

2. Scatter the potato slices over the celery and arrange the crisp squid around.

3. Remove the fish from the oven, drain on kitchen towel and place in the middle of the plate.

4. Finish with the bisque sauce and sprigs of chervil.

Pan-fried brill with potato gnocchi, Norfolk mussels, carrot & ginger stew and fresh coriander

The start of spring can still be quite cold, but hopefully sunny cold. Not much of the new season vegetables are out yet, but it is the time of year that you want fresh, light flavours – the short winter days are on their way out, as have all of the root vegetables. This is a lovely fresh, zingy dish that is still warming, and a nod to the things to come as more and more spring vegetables start to come on to the market.

Serves: 4

For the potato gnocchi:
150g Mashed potato (see Basic Recipes)
25g 'OO' flour
1 Egg yolk
1 Egg
5g Olive oil
10g Cheddar cheese
Table salt

1. Heat the mashed potato in the microwave.

2. Place all of the ingredients into a large bowl and cut through with a metal spoon in the same manner that you would cut/mix a cake recipe. When a uniform dough is achieved, on a well-floured board roll the dough to a long sausage shape. Cut at equal intervals along the sausage to form the gnocchi. Using a well-floured fork, gently press into each parcel to give a corrugated surface on the top of each dumpling.

3. In a pan of boiling (well-seasoned) water, blanch the gnocchi. As they start to float, scoop them out with a slotted spoon on to a well-oiled tray. Allow to cool on the tray and reserve for later.

For the Norfolk mussels, carrot & ginger stew:
1kg Mussels
3 Carrots
3cm Piece fresh ginger
1 Onion
Red chilli
50g Olive oil
200g Martini Extra Dry

1. Pick through the mussels. Discard any that are open or have cracked or broken shells, then wash in cold water.

2. Peel the carrot, ginger, onion and chilli and cut to 5mm dice. In a large pan, sweat them in a good lug of olive oil. After 1 minute, add the mussels and the Martini. Cook altogether with a lid on until all of the mussels have opened. Tip the stew through a colander.

3. In a clean pan reduce the cooking liquid to about 100ml.

4. As the liquid is reducing, pick the mussels from the shell. Discard the shell and keep the meat and vegetables together.

5. When the liquid has reduced remove from the heat.

Other ingredients:
4 x 150g Portions brill (skin removed)
8 Sticks of bok choy
Soy sauce
½ Bunch dill, chopped
½ Bunch chives, chopped
Coriander cress

1. In a hot pan, cook the brill until golden brown. Reduce the heat and let the fish finish slowly.

2. In a separate pan, over a gentle heat in a little oil, fry the gnocchi until golden. Finish under the grill.

3. Steam the bok choy in a little water in a pan with a lid on until just cooked. Season with soy sauce. Remove from the pan and drain on kitchen paper.

4. Reheat the mussel liquid and add the mussels and vegetables. When the stew is hot, add the chopped dill and chives.

5. Place two pieces of bok choy in the centre of each plate and place the brill on top. Arrange five gnocchi around the plate with a little pile of the mussel stew in between. Pour any excess sauce over the fish.

6. Finish the plate with a few leaves of coriander cress.

Rump of dry-aged Hereford beef, with little cottage pie, chargrilled leeks, celeriac & red wine

As with all of the ingredients at Albert's Table, I don't like waste, none more so than beef. Good quality beef is such a treat, but it is also expensive. It is important that there is no waste and that the customers get to enjoy every morsel.

We buy whole rumps of Hereford beef – this is a rare breed of cow that produces wonderful, full-flavoured, tender meat. Quality beef should feel a little greasy to the touch and not be at all wet. There should also be lots of white flecks through it – this is the fat marbling that is so important to the juiciness of a piece of meat.

When preparing the rump there are always little pieces of beef that are too small for a portion and there is also the suet – the two ingredients for perfect minced beef!

Serves: 6

For the beef:
*6 x 170g Portions Hereford
beef rump
1 tbsp Roasted garlic pulp
(see Basic Recipes)
6 Sprigs picked thyme
50g Olive oil*

1. Season the beef all over with salt and pepper and allow to sit at room temperature for 25 minutes.

2. Mix the roasted garlic pulp, picked thyme and olive oil. Dry the beef with kitchen towel and then brush over the garlic-thyme mix. Allow to marinate on a plate until you are ready to cook.

For the cottage pie filling:
*50g Dripping
500g Minced beef
Thyme
1 Bay leaf
2 Small onions
2 Large turnips
2 Carrots
4 Sticks celery
200g Red wine sauce (see
Basic Recipes)
5g Cabernet sauvignon red
wine vinegar*

1. You can prepare the cottage pie filling the day before cooking. On a high heat, melt the dripping in a heavy bottom pan. When it is just smoking, add the minced beef and brown all over.

2. Make a bouquet garni with the thyme and the bay. Dice the onion, turnip, carrot and celery stalks to 5mm dice and add to the mince. Season the mix and continue to cook for only a minute or two.

3. Tip the mix into a colander, allowing all of the fat to run out, and then return the meat and vegetables to the pan. Add the red wine sauce and cook out, uncovered, until the mix is thick and full of flavour. Adjust the seasoning and add the vinegar at this point. This mix will be better the next day, so at this point refrigerate.

For the mash topping:
500g Dry mash (see Basic Recipes)
25g Butter
1 Egg yolk
4g Sea salt
4g White pepper

1. Heat the mash in the microwave and put into a food processor. Add the butter and egg yolk, salt and pepper. The potato must be hot, otherwise it will go thick and gluey.

2. Transfer the potato to a piping bag with a star nozzle.

3. Keep warm until needed.

For the chargrilled leeks and shallots:
3 Banana shallots
2 Leeks (white only)
Maldon sea salt

1. Cut the shallots in half (skin on). Wash the leeks and cut in half lengthways. Season both liberally with sea salt and then steam until cooked (about 5 minutes).

2. Allow to rest at room temperature then cut the leeks into three equal-sized pieces.

For the celeriac purée:
1 Celeriac
200g Whipping cream
Salt and pepper, to season

1. Cut the outer from the celeriac and roughly dice. Transfer to a suitable pan and add the cream and seasoning. Bring up to the simmer and cook out until the celeriac is very soft.

2. Pass the mix through a colander, reserving the liquid. Put the celeriac into a liquidiser and blend until smooth, letting it down with the reserved cream until a thick purée is achieved. Adjust the seasoning, and then pass through a fine sieve. Return to a small pan with a lid on, and keep warm until needed.

Other ingredients:
8 Potato cages (see Basic Recipes)
500g Red wine sauce (see Basic Recipes)

1. Cook the beef on a chargrill, turning every 30 seconds or so, so that it cooks evenly. If using a temperature probe, the centre wants to reach 56ºC for medium rare. Rest the beef in a warm place with foil over for 3 or 4 minutes.

2. Reheat the leeks and the shallots on the chargrill

3. As the beef is cooking, reheat the mince in a pan.

4. Bring the sauce to the boil.

5. When everything is nearly ready, place the potato cages on a baking sheet and fill each one with the mince. Carefully pipe the potato on top and then slide under the grill. Grill the little cottage pies until the potato is golden brown and crisp to the touch.

6. On a warm plate, using a spoon swipe the celeriac purée along one side and place a cottage pie in the middle. Carve the beef across the grain and fan it out along the plate. Finish with a shallot, two pieces of leek and a good splash of red wine sauce.

"As with all of the ingredients at Albert's Table, I don't like waste, none more so than beef. Good quality beef is such a treat, but it is also expensive. It is important that there is no waste and that the customers get to enjoy every morsel."

Grilled leg of Colne Valley hogget with crushed new potatoes, rainbow chard, olives & mint

Hogget is sheep that is between one and two years old. Under one and it is lamb, over one and it is mutton. I like to serve hogget at the beginning of the year, just before the spring lamb is available. Hogget has had time to develop flavour and is still wonderfully tender. We buy ours from the Colne Valley pastures where they have the freedom to roam and graze naturally.

I would describe rainbow chard as a cross between rhubarb and celery; it has its own very distinct flavour.

Marinating any meat adds a contrast between the outside and the inside, none more so than lamb and hogget though.

Serves: 6

For the hogget:
½ Bunch rosemary
2 tbsp Roasted garlic pulp
(see Basic Recipes)
Zest of 2 lemons
Olive oil
Maldon sea salt
1 Leg of hogget (bones removed)

1. The day prior to cooking, chop the rosemary and mix with the garlic, lemon zest and enough olive oil to make a thick paste. Crush the sea salt in a pestle and mortar and then season the leg of hogget all over on both sides, almost massaging it in with your hands. Lightly cover the meat and leave overnight in the fridge.

2. On the day of cooking, pre-heat the oven to 150ºC.

3. Place the hogget on a roasting rack and lightly cover with foil. Cook in the oven until it reaches 60ºC (this will take between 1-2 hours depending on the size of the leg).

4. When cooked, allow the leg to rest for 30 minutes lightly covered with foil. During the resting, leave a thermometer in the thickest part of the joint, it should continue to "cook" for about 10 minutes after you take it out of the oven, and ideally reach 65ºC before it starts to cool down.

For the green herb salsa:
½ Bunch flat leaf parsley
½ Bunch basil
½ Bunch mint
½ Bunch tarragon
2 Green chillies (seeds removed)
2 Garlic cloves
2 Boquerone anchovies
2g Red wine vinegar
1-2 tsp Dijon mustard
Salt and pepper
Extra virgin olive oil

1. Blend all of the ingredients, except the olive oil, to a fine paste.

2. Slowly add the oil until a thick sauce consistency is achieved.

3. Adjust the seasoning to taste.

Grilled leg of Colne Valley hogget with crushed new potatoes, rainbow chard, olives & mint (continued)

For the new potatoes:

600g Kentish new potatoes
50g Slightly salted butter
50g Lilliput capers
50g Kalamata olives (stone removed and cut into quarters)

1. Wash the potatoes and cook in seasoned water – taste the water, it should taste well-seasoned. If you get the water right then the potatoes will be perfectly seasoned all the way through when they are cooked.

2. When the potatoes are cooked, remove the pan from the heat and allow them to cool in the water. When the spuds are cool enough to handle, using a small paring knife, scrape away the skin and discard it. Pop the clean potatoes back into the water until you are ready to serve up.

Other ingredients:

24 Stems rainbow chard, ends trimmed and washed
600g Lamb sauce (see Basic Recipes)

1. Heat a chargrill.

2. Char the lamb on all sides, turning every 30 seconds or so, until it is marked all over – the most glorious smells will be filling the kitchen.

3. Heat a heavy-based sauté pan over a high heat, add the butter, and let it cook until it is golden brown. At this point add the drained potatoes, capers and olives. Turn the heat down and using a fork, crush and turn the spuds – be careful not to make mash.

4. In a pan of salted boiling water, cook the rainbow chard for 2 minutes, or until the stalks are tender. Drain them off and toss in a little olive oil and black pepper.

To serve:

1. Using a ring, spoon the potato mix onto the plate and place four stems of chard next to the potato mix.

2. Carve the lamb and brush over with the green herb salsa, place this over the potatoes and finish with lamb sauce.

Rhubarb pavlova with pistachio

Rhubarb is utterly delicious, but so rarely utilised other than for crumbles. I think of rhubarb as very British, and this dessert is a nice little celebration of rhubarb and many presentations of it.

There will be more rhubarb here than is needed for the recipe, but you need lots of the cooking syrup. At the restaurant, we use the extra rhubarb for crumbles on Sunday.

Most of the work for this dish needs to be done the day before, making it very easy on the day you want to eat.

Serves: 8

For the meringue:
90g Water
300g Sugar
135g Egg whites

1. Pre-heat the oven to 90°C.

2. In a heavy-bottomed pan bring the water and the sugar to the boil. Using a sugar thermometer, allow the syrup to reach 110°C. At this point start whisking the egg whites in a food mixer to form a soft peak meringue. When the sugar reaches 121°C, remove from the heat, turn the mixer to the lowest speed and slowly pour into the meringue mixture.

3. Continue to mix until completely cold (approximately 15 minutes). You should have a glossy thick meringue.

4. Line a baking sheet with baking paper and, using a large spoon, 'plop' 12 piles of meringue on. Clean the spoon and, using kitchen towel, lightly rub with vegetable oil (the oil will stop the spoon sticking to the meringue). Using the back of the spoon, push into each mound of meringue to form a neat shape.

5. Place the baking tray at the bottom of the oven and cook until crisp on the outside. There is no hard and fast rule for how long this will take, but at least 1 hour.

6. Use some of the extra meringues that are on the baking sheet as a tester – eat one. If it is crisp on the outside but soft in the middle, they are ready to come out. If not, leave them in a bit longer – and enjoy another tester in half an hour or so!

For the rhubarb:
1kg Rhubarb (well washed, leaves removed)
330g Sugar
Zest of 2 oranges
50g Water

1. Cut the rhubarb to just fit a large casserole dish. Add all of the ingredients and cook in the same oven as the meringue, but on the top shelf. Rhubarb can be a bit tricky to cook consistently, hence the large quantity. It will overcook very quickly so check it after 20 minutes. You are looking for it to be cooked through, but with a little bite.

2. When ready it will be swimming in all of its juices. Remove from the oven and allow to cool.

3. When cool enough to handle, cut into 1cm chunks, return to the cooking syrup and chill over night.

Rhubarb pavlova with pistachio (continued)

For the rhubarb sauce:
200g Rhubarb syrup
25g Arrowroot

1. Dissolve the arrowroot in about 50g of the rhubarb syrup.

2. Bring the rest of the syrup to the boil and whisk in the arrowroot paste. Bring back to the boil and cook out for 2 or 3 minutes. Remove from the heat, pass through a fine sieve and cool in the fridge.

3. After a couple of hours, the sauce will be cold and will have set. Transfer it to a food processor and blend to a smooth sauce. Pour into a squeeze bottle and store in the fridge until needed.

For the rhubarb sorbet:
Rhubarb syrup
Lemon juice

1. Add a few drops of lemon juice to the remaining rhubarb syrup and churn in an ice cream machine. Store in the freezer until needed.

For the fool:
400g Whipping cream
2 Vanilla pods
400g Natural yoghurt
200g Rhubarb chunks

1. In a large bowl whisk the whipping cream and vanilla seeds to stiff peaks. Fold in the yoghurt and rhubarb and store in the fridge until ready to serve.

2. The fool will only last an hour before it starts to drop and become liquid again, so don't make it too far in advance. Don't be surprised that the fool is not sweet; I don't add any sugar because there is so much in the meringue that when you eat the two together the balance is correct, and not oversweet.

Other ingredients:
50g Pistachio nuts (roasted)

To serve:

1. Place a meringue in the middle of each plate. In the middle of each, place a small scoop of rhubarb sorbet. On top of the sorbet pile up the fool – don't worry if it cascades down the sides – and then sprinkle the whole thing with pistachio nuts.

2. Squeeze the rhubarb sauce over and around the plate.

Carrot cake with white chocolate mousse & poppy seed allumette

I love carrot cake, but I hate the cream cheese topping it is traditionally served with, it is too sweet and sickly – it's a bit of an insult to cheese too… but let's not get started on that.

I want to be able to serve a carrot cake that you can taste, with a refined topping – and what is more refined than white chocolate mousse? Allumette are puff pastry sticks coated in royal icing and baked. For any one that needs a sweet kick, this is it.

Serves: 6

For the carrot cake:
90g Flour
1g Pimento
2g Bicarbonate of soda
1g Baking powder
100g Demerara sugar
75g Vegetable oil
2 Eggs
1g Maldon sea salt
120g Grated carrot

1. Pre-heat the oven to 170°C.

2. Place all of the ingredients into a food mixer, and beat together.

3. Line six silicone muffin moulds with butter, and then dust with flour.

4. Spoon the mix into each mould to fill to two-thirds.

5. Bake in the oven for 20 minutes.

6. Leave to cool in the moulds.

For the white chocolate mousse:
100g Milk
100g Double cream
20g Sugar
2 Egg yolks
300g White chocolate
225g Double cream

1. Bring the milk and cream to the boil. In a separate bowl, whisk the sugar and the egg yolks. Beat the two together and cook out until the custard thickens and will coat the back of a spoon.

2. Remove from the heat, add the white chocolate and whisk for two more minutes. Pour the white chocolate custard through a fine sieve and allow to cool in a large bowl, but don't put it in the fridge.

3. When it has cooled to 20°C, whisk the double cream to soft peaks and fold into the white chocolate custard. Refrigerate to set.

For the allumette:
200g Puff pastry (see Basic Recipes)
50g Egg whites
250g Icing sugar
Juice of ¼ lemon
1 tbsp Poppy seeds

1. Roll the puff pasty out to a thickness of 2mm and pop it into the freezer still on the chopping board.

2. Whisk the egg white, icing sugar and lemon juice to a smooth paste and spread an even layer over the puff pastry that is in the freezer. Sprinkle over the poppy seeds, and return the whole thing back to the freezer to firm up for about 25 minutes.

3. Pre-heat the oven to 150°C (preferably, no fan).

4. Remove the chopping board from the freezer and cut the pastry into long thin triangle strips and place onto a baking sheet. Bake the allumette for about 15 minutes or until they are crisp.

For the carrot purée:
500g Select carrots, finely chopped
125g Slightly salted butter
1 Star anise
9g Sugar
150g Water

1. Place all of the ingredients into a pan with a lid and cook out on a low heat for about 20 minutes, or until the carrots are very soft.

2. Transfer to a food processor and blend until smooth. Pass through a fine sieve into a squeeze bottle.

3. Store in the fridge until required.

To serve:

1. Using an apple corer, make a hole in centre of each carrot cake and fill with carrot purée.

2. Place a cake in the centre of each plate and dot more purée around each cake.

3. Drag a warm spoon through the white chocolate mousse to form a neat scoop to place on top of each cake. Rest an allumette up against the mousse.

May
June

Shortcrust tart of Dorset crab, rouille dressing
& fine leaves

Poached organic salmon with crushed peas, mint
& Jersey curd

Cornish mackerel with black olive tapenade and
English runner beans

Slow-roast belly of Old Spot pork with gallette potato,
local bacon & glazed gem lettuce

Grilled sea bass & brown shrimps with potato pancake,
cauliflower, sage & hazelnut butter

Spinach & ricotta tortellini with new season vegetables,
herb dressing & Old Winchester crisps

Loin of dry-aged Hereford beef with tartiflette potato
(ham), parsley crusted mushroom, red wine & watercress

Roast loin (& stuffing) of Old Spot pork with grilled
new potatoes, asparagus, peas & crackling

Crème caramel soufflé with golden raisins, raisin purée,
caramel sauce & vanilla ice cream

Cherry & almond flaky pastry tart with fresh cherries
& set custard

Shortcrust tart of Dorset crab, rouille dressing & fine leaves

Crab tart was on my very first menu, and has not really ever come off. In the early days, I used to try to tweak it or refine it, but always reverted to the original recipe and presentation. The dish is made up of three utterly delicious components that just go so well together: crumbly short pastry; warm crabmeat custard; and a saffron mayonnaise.

At the restaurant, we use live crabs, cook them and then pick them, but you can buy very good quality handpicked crab from a fishmonger. I would not advise using pasteurised crabmeat, though, as it will have lost its lovely fresh sweetness.

A Provençal sauce/dressing is not dissimilar in consistency to mayonnaise. Traditionally thickened with breadcrumbs, I prefer to thicken by emulsifying egg yolks and a blend of oils. Rouille is a traditional accompaniment to fish and should be well-flavoured with saffron and garlic. Don't be put off by the anchovies, as many people are – the little fish add a fresh seasoning without being 'fishy'.

Makes: 1 x 9-inch tart, 10 slices

You will need:
Shortcrust pastry
(see Basic Recipes)

Ingredients
300g Picked white crabmeat
5 Egg yolks
280g Double cream
94g Crème fraîche
Pinch of cayenne
112g Brown crabmeat
4g Maldon sea salt
Pepper

For the rouille dressing:
2 Egg yolks
2 Cooked egg yolks (from hard boiled eggs; cooked and chilled)
¼ tsp Tomato purée
8 Anchovies
½ tsp Saffron
Lemon juice, to taste
1 tbsp English mustard
1 Garlic clove
4 Drops tabasco
125g Olive oil
125g Vegetable oil

1. Press the shortcrust pastry into a tart tin and blind bake (see Basic Recipes).

1. To make the rouille dressing, blend all the ingredients – apart from the oils – in a food processor. Add the oils in a thin stream, as you would to make mayonnaise. Adjust the seasoning and spiciness as desired.

2. Wash your hands thoroughly. Crab has lots of tiny filaments in it, so pick through the white meat on a flat tray with your fingers.

3. In a food processor that has a temperature setting, blitz the other ingredients to 50°C. If your food processor does not have a temperature setting, warm all of the ingredients to blood temperature before blending.

4. Pass through a chinois then fold in the white meat. With a nice clean finger, have a taste and adjust the seasoning to your liking.

5. Pour into the pre-baked tart ring and cook at 120°C for about 25 minutes. The time will vary massively depending on the oven that you have. The best way to check if the tart is cooked is to open the oven door, and very gently give the tart a little nudge. It's ready when it has the slightest wobble to it – like a firm jelly might just shudder before returning to its original position.

6. Allow to rest in a warm place for 30 minutes before serving with a good dollop of the dressing and young, crisp salad leaves.

Poached organic salmon with crushed peas, mint & Jersey curd

Peas are one of the first spring vegetables to come through, and they are available at the same time that salmon is bang in season. I don't think that it is any coincidence that foods of the same season accompany each other very well.

This is a very simple starter that relies heavily on really good quality ingredients. Jersey curd is a beautiful ingredient. It is produced at the start of the cheese process when curds are separated from the whey of Jersey cows. The curd is then hung in a muslin cloth to dry – that's it, a very young creamy cheese.

Serves: 6

For the Jersey curd:
200g Jersey curd
100g Whipping cream
Salt and pepper
Lemon juice

1. Lightly whisk the curd and the cream together and fold in seasoning to taste. Add a little lemon juice if a bit of acidity is required.

2. Store in the fridge until needed.

For the pea and mint crush:
300g Fresh peas
30g Extra virgin olive oil
15g Fresh mint leaves

1. Cook the peas in boiling water until soft. As soon as they are cooked, refresh by transferring them into a pan of ice cold water.

2. Drain the peas and put into a food processor with the olive oil and seasoning. Blend to a chunky paste.

3. Chop the mint by hand as finely as you can and stir through the paste. Store at room temperature until required.

For the focaccia tuile:
Focaccia (see Basic Recipes)
Olive oil

1. Pre-heat oven to 160°C.

2. Slice the focaccia as thinly as possible – you should be able to see through it (it may help to semi-freeze the bread first before trying to cut it). You will need only one slice per plate, but I advise always cook extra as some will get broken.

3. Lay the bread slices on a baking sheet, saturate with olive oil and bake in the oven for 15 minutes until they are golden and crisp – be careful when removing them from the oil as they will be hot and very delicate!

4. Drain on kitchen paper until ready to serve.

For the salmon:

500g Salmon fillet
Sea salt
Black pepper
Extra virgin olive oil
1kg Nage (see Basics Recipes)

1. Season the salmon all over, rub with a little olive oil and leave to rest for 20 minutes.

2. In a shallow pan bring the nage to the simmer and adjust the seasoning – there needs to be enough stock so the fish will be completely submerged when it goes in.

3. Turn off the heat and let the nage cool to 70°C. At this point add the salmon and let the heat of the nage gently cook the fish. Allow the salmon to rest in the stock until you serve.

Other ingredients:

Pea shoots

To serve:

1. Spread the bottom of the plates with the pea mix. Drain the salmon on kitchen paper and break into six pieces, re-season and place on top of the peas.

3. Using two teaspoons, drop a quenelle of Jersey curd on each piece of salmon.

4. Finish the plate with pea shoots and the focaccia tuile.

Cornish mackerel with black olive tapenade and English runner beans

Mackerel is such a versatile fish and has a sweet, fresh taste of the sea. Hot or cold, it is utterly delicious. It must be really fresh though! This dish features three different preparations of mackerel, all brought together on one plate.

Serves: 8

For the smoked mackerel rillettes:
6 Mackerel fillets (150g each)
1 tbsp Crème fraîche
½ Bunch dill
3cm Horseradish root
Zest of 2 lemons
Juice of 1 lemon
Salt and pepper

Smoking:

1. In the kitchen, we have an old, battered fish smoker. They are not very expensive, but work brilliantly. The method we employ for smoking the fish is a bit dated and rustic, but to be honest, I wouldn't have it any other way.

2. It's easy; soak wood chips of your choice in water for 24 hours, then scatter them on the base of the smoker. Put the whole smoker on a solid top stove and 'cook' until it is bellowing smoke. Lay your fish on the smoking rack then, as quickly as possible, whip the lid off of the smoker, drop the smoking rack in, and put the lid back on. In a domestic kitchen you will need to open the back door to avoid triggering your smoke alarm!

3. Fish needs to smoke on full heat for exactly 30 seconds. Then you take the smoker off the heat (keeping the lid firmly in place) and leave it to rest somewhere for about 30 minutes while the smoke works its wonders.

4. When you remove the lid the mackerel should be just cooked and have a wonderful, smoky aroma.

5. Remove the skin from the fish and you are ready to make the rillettes.

6. Using the largest bowl that you have, mix all the ingredients together. Be gentle – you do not want mackerel paste. And feel free to vary the quantities of the flavourings to suit your tastebuds.

For the soused mackerel:
8 Mackerel fillets
100g Olive oil
200g Chardonnay vinegar
2 tbsp Pink peppercorns
1 Shallot
Juice & zest of 4 limes
Juice & zest of 2 lemons
1 Bunch dill
6 Coriander seeds (toasted)

1. The acidity in the marinade cures the fish. It is important to use good quality vinegar, which won't overpower the flavour. You can use the marinade a couple of times.

2. Cut the fillets in half lengthways, then trim each to 5cm. Warm all ingredients except lemon and lime juice and zest, dill and coriander seeds to 40°C, then add the remaining ingredients.

3. Souse half the mackerel pieces for 3 hours, then remove from the liquid. The remaining mackerel pieces will be grilled later.

For the tapenade:

300g Olives
75g Capers
5g Garlic
2 Anchovy fillets
100g Olive oil

1. Blend all of the ingredients in a food processor. You should have a thick paste.

For the runner beans:

8 Runner beans
1 Anchovy fillet
Few drops of house dressing
(see Basic Recipes)
¼ Red onion, very fine dice

1. Blanch the beans in boiling salted water for 5 minutes then refresh in iced water. Remove the tough string down each side. Dry and cut to 5cm matchsticks.

2. Chop up the anchovy and mix with the dressing and half of the red onion. Reserve with the beans to finish later.

Garnish ingredients:

8 Pieces semi-dried tomato
Freeze-dried tomato powder
8 Sprigs chervil

To serve:

1. Set out eight room temperature plates and sprinkle a line of freeze-dried tomato powder down the middle of each.

2. Start to grill the reserved mackerel strips, skin-side up. When they are warm to the touch on the flesh side they are ready.

3. While the mackerel is grilling, mix the runner beans with the anchovy and red onion dressing and season well.

4. At one edge of each plate put a little pile of the runner beans. A finger-width space from the beans, place a little quenelle of tapenade and top with a piece of soused mackerel.

5. A finger-width space from the tapenade, place a quenelle of rillettes and top with a tomato segment.

6. When the grilled mackerel is ready, pop it onto the runner beans. Finish the plate with some chervil sprigs.

"Mackerel is such a versatile fish and has a sweet, fresh taste of the sea. Hot or cold, it is utterly delicious. It must be really fresh though! This dish features three different preparations of mackerel, all brought together on one plate."

Slow-roast belly of Old Spot pork with gallette potato, local bacon & glazed gem lettuce

Pork belly is a beautiful cut of meat, tender, juicy and full of flavour. I do like to use a lot of pork at the restaurant simply because most people seldom experience really good quality pork. The best pork that I have ever tasted is the Middle White from Huntsham Farm in Gloucestershire, it's not cheap, but by gosh it's worth it. When Richard (the farmer) phones up to see if we want half a pig I invariably find myself saying yes – even if pork is not on the menu!

Serves: 8

For the pork belly:
2kg Middle White or Old
Spot pork belly
Vegetable oil
Maldon sea salt
20g Coriander seeds
20g Fennel seeds
5g Chilli flakes
10g Roasted garlic pulp (see
Basic Recipes)

1. Pre-heat the oven to 150ºC.

2. Remove the skin from the pork. Cross-hatch the fat with a sharp knife and rub all over with vegetable oil and Maldon sea salt. Allow the pork to rest for 15 minutes to let the seasoning penetrate the meat.

3. Lightly grind the coriander seeds, fennel seeds, chilli flakes and garlic pulp in a pestle and mortar and rub into the skin side of the pork. Place the pork on a roasting rack with the tray underneath half filled with water and cook until a skewer shows no resistance when pushed into the meat – about 2½ hours. The pork should be golden brown and very tender – cut a sliver off and eat it if you are not sure.

3. When cooked, remove from the oven and allow to rest for 20 minutes before serving.

For the carrot purée:
250g Select carrots, finely
chopped
125g Butter
1 Star anise
3g Salt
2g Sugar
75g Water

1. Place all of the ingredients into a pan with a lid and cook out on a low heat for about 20 minutes, or until the carrots are very soft.

2. Remove the star anise and transfer the rest to a food processor and blend until smooth. Pass through a fine sieve and reserve until needed.

For the gem lettuce:
4 Baby gem lettuce
Salt and pepper
100g Butter
Chicken stock (see Basic
Recipes)
200g Smoked bacon lardons

1. Wash and cut the baby gem in half lengthways. Trim off any old leaves and the discoloured stalk and season on both sides.

2. In a wide, shallow pan, melt the butter. When foaming, add the gem, cut side down, in a single layer. Cook until slightly coloured.

2. Add the chicken stock (to just cover the lettuce), smoked bacon, and bring to the boil. Cook with a lid on for about 5 minutes until the gem is cooked and tender and allow to rest in the stock until ready.

For the gallette potato:

1kg Potatoes
Vegetable oil
Table salt

1. Pre-heat oven to 160°C.

2. Wash and peel the potatoes. Slice on a mandolin wafer thin and then cut out with a 50mm cutter. Allow 15 slices per portion.

3. On greaseproof paper arrange the potatoes into a rosette. Brush with oil and season with table salt. Place the rosettes on a baking sheet with a silicone mat over the top. Cook for 20 minutes, then chill before removing from the tray.

Other ingredients:

600g Pork sauce (see Basic Recipes)
Flat parsley
Grain mustard

1. Shallow fry the potato gallettes in vegetable oil until golden and crisp, and reheat the carrot purée in a pan.

2. Place the gem pan on a high heat and reduce the stock to a nice sticky glaze and finish with chopped parsley and grain mustard.

3. Carve the pork into three pieces per portion and flash under the grill to get it piping hot again.

4. Swipe carrot purée trough the centre of each plate and place the pork at right angles to the purée. Gut the gallette in half and lean it between the pork. Pour on the sauce and finish with the glazed gem and bacon.

Grilled sea bass & brown shrimps with potato pancake, cauliflower, sage & hazelnut butter

I am not a fan of truffle oil, it tastes of chemicals and very rarely like a real truffle. There is an exception though, well two actually. Cauliflower and celeriac purée. A couple of drops of truffle oil to either of these purées really lift the finished product to new heights, just don't overdo it. Think of the truffle oil almost as a seasoning.

Serves: 6

For the potato pancake:
250g Dry mash
40g 'OO' flour
4g Table salt
8g Cheddar cheese
1 Egg yolk
1 Egg
75g Crème frâiche

1. Gently whisk all of the ingredients together until smooth – make sure the mash is hot, otherwise it will go gluey. Check the seasoning and transfer to a piping bag.

For the cauliflower purée:
1 Cauliflower
200g Whipping cream
Maldon sea salt
Truffle oil

1. Remove the core from the cauliflower and slice the florets as finely as possible.

2. Add the cauliflower and seasoning to a saucepan with the cream and cook out over a medium heat with a lid on until the cauliflower is very tender.

3. Blend the mix in a food processor until very smooth and add a few drops of truffle oil. Adjust the seasoning as required and pass through a fine sieve.

For the vichy vegetables:
150g Carrot
80g Celery
80g Leek
200g Nage (see Basic Recipes)
50g Unsalted butter
10g Sugar
40g Brown shrimps
40g Toasted hazelnuts
½ Bunch chopped sage
½ Bunch flat parsley, chopped

1. Wash, peel and cut the vegetables above to a neat uniform dice – the weights above are the prepared weights.

2. Heat the nage, butter and sugar in a pan, add the vegetables and cook out for about 4 minutes with a lid on over a high heat – the veg should be just cooked. Add the shrimps, hazelnuts and the herbs and mix all together.

For the fish:
6 x 150g Sea bass fillets
Knob of butter
Lemon juice

1. In a warm pan on a medium heat with minimal oil, cook the fish on the skin side until crisp. Remove the pan from the heat, flip the fillets onto the flesh side, add a knob of butter and a squeeze of lemon juice.

2. Wipe a wide non-stick pan with vegetable oil and pipe in six little pancakes. Cook over a gentle heat until they just start to colour around the edges and then transfer the pan to the bottom of the grill. Cook out for 3 or 4 minutes until the pancakes are puffed up and firm.

3. Reheat the cauliflower purée.

4. To serve, spoon the cauliflower purée into the middle of each plate and rest a pancake on top – push it into the purée gently to stop the pancake sliding around.

5. Spoon the vegetables around the pancake and finish with the fish.

Spinach & ricotta tortellini with new season vegetables, herb dressing & Old Winchester crisps

In the restaurant, we have many dishes that consist of lovely vegetable preparations; with a couple of tweaks they make a lovely vegetarian dish in their own right. This is a prime example. The sea bass dish on the previous page is garnished with new season vegetables, so we use many of the same vegetables to make this tortellini dish.

Serves: 8

For the spinach & ricotta tortellini:
Pasta dough (see Basic Recipes)
225g Spinach
112g Ricotta (hung weight)
20g Butter
1 Egg
1 Egg yolk
Nutmeg
42g Flour
Salt and pepper
200g Couscous

1. On the day prior to cooking, take 200g ricotta and hang it in a muslin cloth overnight. You want to use 112g.

2. On the day of cooking, wash the spinach and wilt in a pan until well cooked. Drain on a cloth and chill in fridge.

3. When cold, roughly chop the spinach and mix with the ricotta, butter, egg, yolk and rasp in some fresh nutmeg. Fold in the flour and adjust the seasoning. Chill and rest the mix.

4. Between two spoons, quenelle the mix and lay on greaseproof paper on a tray. You need 24 quenelles in total.

5. Roll out the pasta as described in the Basic Recipes section and roll it down to number 3 on the pasta machine. Using a 40mm cutter, cut out 24 pasta discs and cover with a damp cloth to stop them drying out.

6. Run one of the pasta discs through the pasta machine on number 1 and lay it across your hand. Spoon one of the quenelles of ricotta mix into the centre of the pasta. Fold the pasta in half to form a semi-circle and gently crimp the two surfaces together, squeezing out all of the air as you go.

7. Take the two ends of the semi-circle of pasta and bring them together and pinch together to finish the tortellini.

8. Tip the couscous on a tray and rest the tortellini on the couscous to prevent it sticking to your work surface. Now repeat for the rest of the pasta and filling.

Spinach & ricotta tortellini with new season vegetables, herb dressing & Old Winchester crisps (continued)

For the vegetables:
150g Carrot
80g Celery
200g Nage (see Basic Recipes)
10g Sugar
50g Unsalted butter
16 Asparagus spears (each cut into 3)
½ Bunch chopped sage
½ Bunch chopped flat parsley
½ Bunch marjoram
Salt and pepper

1. Wash, peel and cut the carrots and celery to neat uniform dice – the weights opposite are the prepared weights.

2. Heat the nage, butter and sugar in a pan, add the vegetables and cook out for about 4 minutes with a lid on over a high heat – the veg should be just cooked. Add the herbs and mix all together. Adjust the seasoning.

For the Winchester crisps:
200g Old Winchester cheese

1. Pre-heat the oven to 160ºC.

2. Line a baking sheet with a silicone mat and, using a 90mm cutter as a template, make 12 discs of grated cheese on the mat. Cook until golden and crisp.

3. Remove from the oven and gently lift from the tray.

To serve:

1. Bring a large pan of well-seasoned water to the boil. Add the tortellini and cook until they float, about 2 minutes.

2. Divide the vegetables into eight warm bowls, drain the pasta from the water with a slotted spoon and place in the centre of the vegetables. Snap the cheese crisps into shards and arrange on the plate.

Loin of dry-aged Hereford beef with tartiflette potato (ham), parsley crusted mushroom, red wine & watercress

I spent a few years living in the Alps, the home of the tartiflette, and have always wanted a version on the menu at the restaurant – of course I have replaced all of the French ingredients with British ones. For anyone that has eaten in the mountains, I hope I have done a great dish justice.

Serves: 8

For the parsley crust:
90g Melted butter
90g Breadcrumbs or brioche
50g Hard cheese
25g Curly parsley
Salt and pepper

1. Prepare the parsley crust the day before by blending all of the ingredients in a food processor.

2. Tip out onto a large chopping board lined with baking paper then place another sheet of paper over the top and roll out to 2mm thickness. Place the whole chopping board in the fridge to allow the crust to set.

For the beef:
2kg Sirloin Hereford beef
Salt and pepper

1. Pre-heat the oven to 150ºC.

2. Season the beef all over. Place on a roasting rack and cook uncovered until the centre of the beef reaches 56ºC on a meat thermometer. Lightly cover with foil and allow to rest whilst everything else is prepared.

For the tartiflette:
1.5kg Maris Piper potatoes
500g Unsliced ham
85g Butter
75g Onion, diced
50g Flour
375g Milk
375g Cream
1 Bay leaf
3 Peppercorns
3 Cloves
100g Baronet cheese, grated
2g English mustard

1. Wash, peel and dice the potatoes into 1cm cubes. Cut the ham to the same size and reserve until later.

2. Melt the butter in a suitable pan, add the onion and cook until soft – don't allow it to colour. Add the flour and cook out for a further 5 minutes.

3. In a separate pan warm the milk, cream, bay, peppercorns and cloves and when simmering, transfer to the flour mix. Whisk until it reaches the boil. Pop a lid on the pan and on the lowest heat cook out for about 40 minutes.

4. Remove from the heat and fold in the grated cheese and mustard.

5. Adjust the seasoning.

Loin of dry-aged Hereford beef with tartiflette potato (ham), parsley crusted mushroom, red wine & watercress (continued)

For the field mushrooms:
8 Field mushrooms
50g Butter
50g White wine
Thyme
Bay leaf
1 tsp Roasted garlic pulp
(see Basic Recipes)

1. Pre-heat the oven to 170ºC.

2. Remove the stalks from the mushrooms and wipe clean with a damp cloth.

3. In a roasting tray melt the butter, wine, herbs and garlic and give them a little mix. Add the mushrooms and coat them in the garlic butter. Season well, cover with foil and bake in the oven for 30 minutes. When cooked, rest with the foil intact to keep all of the juices in the dish.

Other ingredients:
8 Potato cages (see Basic Recipes)
1 Bunch chopped chives
8 Bunch watercress
500g Spinach
600g Red wine sauce (see Basic Recipes)

1. Heat some vegetable oil in a heavy bottom pan. When it is hot, colour the cooked beef on all sides.

2. Cook the potato dice in boiling water – be careful as they will only take a couple of minutes, and believe me that it is very upsetting to spend an age cutting lovely little dice, only to overcook the lot and have to start again! Pass into a colander and then add to the hot cheese sauce with the ham. Warm all together then remove from the heat and finish with chopped chives.

3. Remove the mushrooms from the oven dish and cut out using a 40mm cutter. Cut the parsley crust to the same size and place one parsley disc onto each mushroom. Pop under the grill to gratinate the parsley

4. Carve the beef.

5. To serve, place a potato cage on each plate and fill with the tartiflette mix. Arrange the spinach next to it with the beef over the top.

6. Perch the gratinated mushroom on the beef and finish with the sauce and a small bunch of watercress.

Roast loin (& stuffing) of Old Spot pork with grilled new potatoes, asparagus, peas & crackling

I utilise the trim from either side of the pork loin to make the stuffing for this dish. Purely by luck the trim from the loin will be about the correct amount to make the stuffing.

Serves: 6

For the pork:
2 kg Old Spot pork loin
Brine (see Basic Recipes)

1. Prepare the pork the day before by removing the skin from the loin. Use this to make the crackling. Cross-hatch the fat with a sharp knife and brine the meat for four hours, then pat dry. Brining pork will help retain all of the natural juiciness of the meat when it is cooked.

2. On the day, pre-heat the oven to 180°C.

3. In a warm pan with a little oil, render the fat side of the pork loin until it just starts to colour. Cover the joint with foil and place the pan in the oven. Cook until the internal temperature reaches 65°C. When cooked, allow the leg to rest for 30 minutes lightly covered with foil. During the resting leave a thermometer in the thickest part of the joint, it should continue to "cook" for about 10 minutes after you take it out of the oven, and ideally reach 67°C before it starts to cool down.

For the pork apricot and pine nut stuffing:
1 Onion
Olive oil
1 tsp Mixed spice
100g Polenta
75g Semi-skimmed milk
300g Minced pork
50g Dried apricot, chopped
25g Toasted pine nuts
1 Bunch sage, roughly chopped

1. Sweat off the onion in a little olive oil and seasoning until they are very soft, then add the mixed spice.

2. Soak the polenta in the milk and add to the cooled onions, along with the pork, apricot, pine nuts and sage. Beat the stuffing mix together in a food mixer. At this point I fry up a bit of the stuffing as a tester to make sure the seasoning is accurate; if not, re-season and test until you are happy.

3. Between a sheet of clingfilm, roll the mix into a long sausage about 3cm in diameter and poach in simmering water for 15 minutes. When cooked, drop into iced water to cool.

For the pea purée:
250g Fresh peas
80g Whipping cream
Salt and pepper, to season

1. Cook the peas in boiling water. When tender, drain off and pour into a food processor. Add the cream and blend until smooth. Adjust the seasoning, pass through a fine sieve and cool in a container sat in iced water – this will help it stay vibrant and green.

Roast loin (& stuffing) of Old Spot pork with grilled new potatoes, asparagus, peas & crackling (continued)

For the pea, onion and wild garlic garnish:

2 Small onions
Olive oil
1kg Fresh peas
250g Wild garlic

1. Slice the onion very fine and cook on a low heat in a little olive oil with a lid on until very tender – this will take about 10 minutes. When the onions are cooked, keep warm until required.

2. To finish, boil the peas until tender then add them to the onions along with the chopped wild garlic. Mix altogether on the heat until the garlic has wilted.

Other ingredients:

Pork sauce (see Basic Recipes)
Crackling (see Basic Recipes)
Grilled potatoes (see Basic Recipes)
6 Asparagus spears

1. While the pork is resting, cut the stuffing into six equal pieces and grill on one side. Pop in the oven to warm through.

2. Steam the asparagus in a steamer or cook in boiling water until just tender.

3. Heat the pea purée and the pork sauce. Carve the pork.

4. To serve, swipe the pea purée around the edge of the plate and pile some of the pea and onion garnish in the middle. Arrange the grilled potatoes next to the peas and place the stuffing at the top of the plate. Lay the pork over the pea mix and finish with crackling and asparagus.

Crème caramel soufflé with golden raisins, raisin purée, caramel sauce & vanilla ice cream

My take on a classic crème caramel. Being a soufflé it is obviously much lighter and a lovely way to finish a meal on a hot summer day.

Serves: 8

For the caramel sauce:
500g Sugar
250g Water
75g Sauternes sweet wine
100g Golden raisins

1. In a heavy-based pan over a high heat, bring the sugar to a golden caramel. As the caramel shows its first whiffs of smoke add the water and whisk to a smooth syrup.

2. Pass through a fine sieve and add the Sauternes wine and the golden raisins.

3. Allow to sit at room temperature until you are ready to serve.

For the soufflé:
315g Rice pudding purée
(see Basic Recipes)
90g Sauternes sweet wine
8 Eggs, separated
125g Sugar

1. Pre-heat the oven to 180°C.

2. Line eight 250ml pudding moulds with butter and then sugar.

3. In a large bowl over simmering water, cook the rice pudding, Sauternes and egg yolks until they start to thicken. This will only take about 5 minutes, but you do need to whisk all of the time.

4, Remove from the heat, reserving the hot water for later.

5. Whisk the egg whites and the sugar to a glossy meringue. Fold this into the rice pudding mixture in three batches – you will find the whites incorporate much easier if you are quite vigorous with the first inclusion, and make sure that the mix is completely homogeneous before adding the next two batches of egg whites.

6. Distribute the soufflé mix carefully between the moulds. Place the moulds into an oven dish and then fill with boiling water to come half way up the moulds. Bake for 8 minutes until well risen and golden, and then remove the baking dish from the oven and allow the soufflés to cool in the water for 10 minutes.

7. After the rest, turn the soufflés out onto greaseproof paper and store in the fridge until ready to serve. The soufflés will keep for about 12 hours in the fridge. After this they will not rise so well when cooked.

For the raisin purée:
125g Water
250g Raisins

1. Bring the water to the boil and then add the raisins. Remove from the heat, cover with a lid and then rest in a warm place for 2 hours – the raisins will absorb all of the water. Blend in a food processor, and then pass through a potato mouli to get it really smooth.

2. Store in the fridge until needed.

Other ingredients:
Vanilla ice cream (see Basic Recipes)
8 x Tuile baskets (see Basic Recipes)

To serve:

1. Pre-heat a baking sheet to 180ºC.

2. Slide the soufflés directly onto the hot baking sheet and re-cook for 7 minutes.

3. Pipe the raisin purée around the rim of the plate and stick a tuile basket onto one of the purée dots. Place a scoop of the vanilla ice cream in the basket.

4. As soon as the soufflé is ready, slide onto the plate and spoon over the golden raisin caramel. Serve straight away.

Cherry & almond flaky pastry tart with fresh cherries & set custard

During the summer months cherries are so juicy, sweet and full of flavour – and they taste so wonderful with almonds. This dish is effectively a Bakewell tart made with cherries instead of raspberries. I used to work with a pastry chef that hated frangipane because it is so 'seventies' and not exciting – but in my mind a good frangipane is unbeatable, even if it is not new or exciting.

Serves: 8

For the cherry & almond tart:
200g Flaky pastry (see Basic Recipes)
190g Butter
190g Sugar
1 tsp Mixed spice
190g Almonds
1 tbsp Flour
3 Eggs
300g Griottine cherries (drained)

1. Pre-heat the oven to 180ºC.

2. Roll out the flaky pastry to line a 20cm x 30cm brownie tin and then rest it in the fridge for 30 minutes.

3. Cream the butter, sugar and mixed spice, then add the almonds and flour (mixing and scraping down as you go). Start to add the eggs one at a time, not adding the next egg until the first has been incorporated.

4. After the last egg has been mixed, gently fold in the cherries. Do not overmix at this point as you don't want to bash the cherries about too much!

5. Pour the mix into the pastry case, level off with a spatula and then sprinkle flaked almonds over the top. Bake in the oven for approximately 30 minutes or until firm to the touch and cooked through.

For the set custard:
210g Double cream
1 Vanilla pod
25g Sugar
3 Egg yolks

1. In a heavy-based pan bring the cream and vanilla to the boil. Whilst the cream is coming up, mix the sugar and egg yolks in large bowl.

2. Add a third of the hot cream into the bowl, whisk it together and then pour it back into the rest of the cream. Cook out to 87ºC, stirring all the time (the mix will have thickened up, and will coat the back of a spoon).

3. Remove from the heat and continue to whisk for at least 3 minutes – this will stop the residual heat of the pan curdling the custard. Pass the custard through a fine sieve into a 2-litre container and chill to set in the fridge. Once set, spoon into a piping bag fitted with a star nozzle.

For the cherry foam:
1kg Fresh cherries
150g Sugar
1 Bunch mint stalks
Lemon juice
4 Leaves gelatine

1. Wash the cherries well in cold water then throw into a large bowl with the sugar and mint stalks. Wrap the whole bowl in clingfilm and sit over a pan of simmering water for 2 hours – it is important that the water is just simmering so that it gently warms up the cherries and they release all of their lovely juices.

2. After 2 hours the bowl should be full of cherries bobbing around in their own juices. Tip the whole lot through a colander sat over a container and let it drip through for about 20 minutes. Add a little lemon juice to taste if needed.

3. Soften the gelatine in cold water and then mix it into 700g of the warm cherry syrup.

4. Fill an espuma gun with the syrup and charge.

Other ingredients:
8 x Tuile baskets (see Basic Recipes)
100g Fresh cherries, seeded and chopped into quarters
8 Sprigs mint

To serve:

1. Divide the fresh cherries between the tuile baskets and pipe the custard mix on top. Take a nice slice of tart and plate it next the tuile basket and finish with the cherry foam and fresh mint.

July
August

Summer gazpacho & basil oil, chilled with tomato sorbet

Little tart of courgette & marjoram with button mushroom
mousse & 8-year-old balsamic vinegar

Smoked ham hock & summer beans with whipped Rosary
goats' cheese, beetroot & chargrilled bruschetta

Oven-baked salmon with a warm salad of new potato, beets
& leek hearts, smoked goats' curd and orange dressing

Pan-fried stone bass with stuffed squid, artichokes & clams

Creedy Carver chicken; roast breast & boudin of leg,
with Anna potato, girolle mushrooms & broad beans

Breast of Creedy Carver duck with Wensleydale
spring greens & Black Combe ham, rosemary
roast potatoes & fresh fig

Kentish raspberries with cottage cheesecake mille feuille
& raspberry sorbet

Vanilla cream with fresh Kentish strawberries
& warm vanilla doughnuts

Apricot-glazed rum baba with orange segments
& Cornish clotted cream

Summer gazpacho & basil oil, chilled with tomato sorbet

I love gazpacho – real gazpacho. This is a dish that is done badly by so many restaurants. Good gazpacho, however, almost makes you feel healthy as you eat/drink it. In the summer the kitchen can get very hot, and this is my drink of choice to cool off and rehydrate. I like to serve it with a tomato sorbet so that it stays ice cold as you eat it and to keep it very fresh tasting – almost like a chilled white wine.

If any recipe relied on fresh, top quality ingredients, it is this. From the vegetables to the oil and the vinegar, make sure you use the best that you can get – it is worth it.

Serves: 8

For the tomato sorbet (makes 2 litres):
100g Water
85g Caster sugar
1.5kg Tomatoes
3 tbsp Extra virgin olive oil
1 Small red onion
1 Sprig thyme
2 Strips orange zest
1½ tsp Salt
8 Basil leaves, finely sliced
1 tsp White wine vinegar
Pinch of cayenne pepper

1. Make a syrup by boiling together the water and the sugar.

2. Cut the tomatoes into quarters, deseed and chop.

3. In a medium pan, heat the oil and add the chopped onion, thyme, orange zest and salt. Over a medium heat, cook without colour.

4. Add a third of the tomatoes and cook out for 5 minutes with the lid on. Remove the lid and cook out to a thick pulp, stirring frequently to stop the tomatoes from burning. Do not be tempted to turn the heat up – this wants to be a steady process that keeps all the sweetness in. Allow to cool.

5. Add all of the other ingredients (the remaining two-thirds of the tomatoes, syrup, basil, white wine vinegar, cayenne and the cooked tomato pulp) to a food processor. Blend on full speed, then pass through a sieve.

6. Chill in the fridge. At this point the sorbet base will keep for three days, so you can get ahead of yourself.

7. On the day you wish to serve, put the filling into an ice cream machine and churn until it is smooth, glossy and firm. Place in the freezer until you are ready to serve.

For the basil oil:
2 Bunches basil
150g Extra virgin olive oil
Maldon sea salt, to taste

1. Pick the leaves from the basil. Using a basket, drop the basil leaves into a pan of boiling water and blanch the leaves for 10 seconds.

2. Remove the basket and drop straight into iced water to refresh. When cool, pat dry on a dishcloth or kitchen towel.

3. In a food processor, blend the basil and olive oil together with a little sea salt. When very smooth, transfer the green oil to a squeeze bottle. Use within 48 hours, otherwise the colour will start to lose its vibrancy.

For the gazpacho:
2 Cucumbers, peeled &
seeded
5 Red peppers
5 Tomatoes
1 Red onion
½ Red chilli
2 Garlic cloves
¼ Bunch basil
100g Cabernet sauvignon
vinegar
50g Olive oil
1g Smoked paprika
10g Maldon sea salt
5g Sugar
Basil cress

1. Roughly chop all of the vegetables and herbs and put into a large bowl with the vinegar, oil and seasonings. This is definitely a job to enjoy with a glass of wine! It does not need to be neat and tidy, and the fresh fragrance of the ingredients will fill your kitchen.

2. Leave to marinate overnight.

3. Blitz in a food processor and pass through a sieve. Keep in the fridge, but eat on the day you make it, whilst it is super fresh.

To serve:

1. Have your serving bowls ready in the freezer. Pour the gazpacho into each bowl. Using an ice-cream scoop, put a neat scoop of sorbet into the middle of each bowl. Dot the basil oil around, and finish with a sprig of basil cress onto the tomato sorbet.

Little tart of courgette & marjoram with button mushroom mousse & 8-year-old balsamic vinegar

A combination of a warm, buttery puff pastry, red onion and courgette tart, served with frozen goats' cheese and a mushroom mousse. This dish is always very popular when we put it on the menu, and it's a vegetarian dish that does not 'seem' to be vegetarian. There are so many interesting flavours and textures that you won't even notice there is no meat or fish!

Serves: 8

For the courgette tarts:
100g Goats' cheese
Puff pastry (see Basic Recipes)

1. Freeze a small log of young goats' cheese. (At the restaurant we use Rosary, but it is personal preference.)

2. Roll out a sheet of puff pastry to about 2mm thick, and about 20cm x 40cm. Prick all over with a folk, wrap in clingfilm, and then return to the fridge to rest.

For the button mushroom mousse:
150g Button mushrooms
400g Double cream
Nutmeg
Salt and pepper, to taste
Lemon juice, to taste

1. Slice the mushrooms. Put them in a pan with half the cream, seasoning and a few rasps of nutmeg. Bring to the boil and cook out for 2 minutes. Squeeze in a few drops of lemon juice to taste. Pass through a sieve and cool in the fridge.

2. When almost set, fold in the other half of the double cream. Check the seasoning.

3. Leave to set in the fridge – this will take a couple of hours.

For the red onion jam:
2 tbsp Coriander seeds
100g Extra virgin olive oil
10 Red onions, peeled and very finely sliced
4 Garlic cloves, finely sliced
Maldon sea salt, to taste
½ Bunch marjoram

1. Toast the coriander seeds under a grill until they just start to smell toasty. If you have never toasted spices before, don't worry – it is very obvious when they are ready.

2. In a large heavy-bottom pan on a medium heat, warm the olive oil. It may look like a lot, but onions cooked in olive oil have a wonderful flavour.

3. Just as the olive oil starts to show the first signs of heat vapour, pour in the onions, garlic, coriander seeds and a good pinch of sea salt. Give it all a good mix to coat the ingredients in the oil. Put a lid on and cook out for 5 minutes.

4. When you take the lid off the onions should have 'dropped' in the pan to about half the volume that they were when you put them in. They should have softened up. Carry on cooking on a medium heat without a lid until all of the liquid has evaporated and you are left with a thick onion jam.

5. Pour the mix onto a tray and allow to cool for 10 minutes.

6. Pick the marjoram leaves from the stalks and mix them through the onions. Spoon all into a container and refrigerate until needed. There should be about 1 litre of onion jam.

Assembling the tarts:

4 Courgettes
Table salt, to taste
A few sprigs rocket cress
A few drops 8-year-old
Balsamic vinegar

1. Pre-heat the oven to 180°C and slide in a roasting tray to get hot.

2. Wash the courgettes and slice on a mandolin about 2mm thick. Each tart needs 15 slices of courgette (120 slices in total). In a large bowl, sprinkle the courgette slices with table salt and leave for 5 minutes. The salt will leach out the water in the courgettes, intensifying their flavour. Drain the liquid off the courgettes and pat them dry on kitchen towel.

3. Remove the pastry from the fridge and cut out eight tart bases with a 9cm cutter. In the centre of each disc, place a little mound of onion jam (leaving a 1cm border of 'un-jammed' pastry). Take the courgettes and layer them up like a rosette all the way around. To experience the full beauty of this tart, you must cook the puff pastry all the way through. The hot tray in the oven will help with this as it will start cooking the puff from underneath as soon as the tarts go into the oven.

4. Brush the courgettes with olive oil (this will stop them burning in the oven). Slide the assembled tarts on to the hot tray in the oven and cook for about 30 minutes. Whilst they are cooking, warm eight plates.

5. When the tarts are crisp remove from the oven, and leave them on the tray to stay warm.

6. Remove the goats' cheese from the freezer and finely grate it over the plates until it looks like a light dusting of snow. Place a tart in the middle of each plate and with a warm spoon make a nice rocher* of mushroom mousse in the middle of each tart. Finish the plate with a few sprigs of rocket cress and a few drops of aged balsamic vinegar.

A one-handed quenelle; a way to give a beautiful oval shape to a soft food.

*Little tart of courgette & marjoram
with button mushroom mousse
& 8-year-old balsamic vinegar*

Smoked ham hock & summer beans with whipped Rosary goats' cheese, beetroot & chargrilled bruschetta

Ham hock is the front leg of a pig and is basically a small ham. When cooked long and slow in stock and a few amaranths, the meat is succulent and juicy with bags of flavour. In this dish, we use the liquid that we cooked the hock in to make a delicious well-seasoned meat jelly.

Serves: 8

For the ham hocks:
1 Ham hock
2kg Water
2kg Chicken stock
2 tsp Juniper berries
2 Sticks celery
1 Onion
1 Carrot
1 Leek
2 Sprigs thyme
1 Bay leaf
1 Sprig rosemary
Gelatine

1. Pre-heat the oven to 120°C.

2. Soak the ham hocks in cold water for 24 hours to remove some of the saltiness.

3. Put all of the ingredients into a pan and bring to the simmer. Place in the oven with a cartouche and lid until falling from the bone, approximately 3 hours. Allow to cool in the stock.

4. When cool enough to handle, remove the hock from the stock and pick away the good meat (discard the bones and gristle). Gently reduce the cooking liquid until it has a good ham flavour and tastes well-seasoned. Ladle the liquid through a muslin cloth and set with gelatine (1 leaf for each 500g of stock).

5. Set out eight serving bowls and, using a 2oz ladle, measure one ladle of jelly per bowl. Transfer the bowls to the fridge to set.

For the ham salad:
10 Runner beans
400g Tin borlotti beans
(cooked)
¼ bunch Flat leaf parsley
1 tbsp Capers

1. Just before serving, mix the ingredients with the picked ham meat.

For the bruschetta:
Focaccia (see Basic Recipes)
Garlic
Extra virgin olive oil

1. Slice the focaccia and rub all over with fresh garlic.

2. On a hot griddle, mark the focaccia on both sides then rub all over with extra virgin olive oil.

Other ingredients:
200g Rosary goats' cheese
20g Whipping cream
Salt and pepper, to season
1 Beetroot (raw)
Splash of red wine vinegar
Chervil, to garnish

1. Beat the goats' cheese with the whipping cream, salt and pepper.

2. With a sharp knife slice the beetroot and then chop those slices into matchsticks. Marinate the beet in a little red wine vinegar.

To serve:

1. Remove the bowls from the fridge and make a neat quenelle of the Rosary goats' cheese in the centre of each bowl.

2. Scatter the salad around the bowl and finish with the beetroot matchsticks and some fresh chervil.

3. Serve with the focaccia on the side.

Oven-baked salmon with a warm salad of new potato, beets & leek hearts, smoked goats' curd and orange dressing

Salmon is an ingredient that used to be very exclusive but is now available very cheaply, thanks mainly to the increase in farming methods.

To have salmon on a menu, it needs to have a point of difference as it is available on just about every menu up and down the country. Wild salmon is an absolute thing of beauty and although we cannot afford the wild specimen at Albert's Table, I do find that organic, or properly loch farmed salmon, a very good alternative. Salmon needs to swim to build up flavour in its flesh.

This dish is essentially a cracking piece of fish with a simple salad of complementing flavours and textures.

Serves: 6

For the smoked goats' curd:
100g Whipping cream
2g Aga aga
4g Maldon smoked sea salt
100g Goats' curd

1. Place the cream, aga aga and sea salt into a pan and bring to the simmer, stirring all of the time. When it reaches 84°C remove from the heat and allow to cool for 5 minutes. Whisk in the curd.

2. Pass through a sieve and store in the fridge until set.

For the orange & white balsamic dressing:
7g Cardamom
4g Coriander seeds
2 sprigs Thyme
160g Extra virgin olive oil
3g Salt
3g Sugar
60g White balsamic
60g Orange juice

1. Lightly toast the cardamom and coriander seeds then lightly blitz in a spice grinder with the thyme.

2. Mix the oil, salt, sugar, white balsamic and orange and blend with a hand blender. Add the spices and bottle up.

For the salad:

4 Leeks (white part only)
2 Cooked beetroot
4 Cooked new potatoes
18 Walnuts

1. Steam the leeks or cook in boiling water if you don't have a steamer. Test for doneness by inserting a sharp paring knife, there should be very little resistance (undercooked 'squeaky' leeks are horrible at the best of times, but more so in a salad when being eaten at room temperature). When the leeks are cooked, allow to cool on a tray. Cut into 15mm logs on the angle – you will need three logs per plate.

2. Slice the beetroot 3mm thick on a mandolin. Cut the slices with a circular cutter to 15mm.

3. Slice the new potatoes to 3mm on a mandolin. Grill on a griddle iron to give nice charred bar marks.

4. In one bowl put the beet slices and some of the dressing. In a separate bowl put the leeks, charred potato, walnuts and some of the dressing. Toss together and allow to mingle.

Other ingredients:

6 portions Salmon (150-200g each)
Salt and pepper, to season
Lemon slices
100g White wine
6 spears Chives
Tarragon
Fennel cress
100g Salmon keta (caviar)

1. Pre-heat the oven to 160ºC.

2. Season the fillets on both sides with salt and pepper. Lightly oil a non-stick pan, just warm it, and place the fish in skin side down. On a medium heat cook on the skin side until golden and crisp. Remove the salmon from the pan.

3. Cover the base of the pan with lemon slices and a good glug of white wine (about 100g). Return the fish to the pan and cover with foil. Bake the whole thing in the oven. The foil will protect the salmon from the heat of the oven, and the wine will gently steam the flesh. How long it takes will depend on the oven that you use. Aim for an internal temperate of 55ºC and then remove from the oven. Leave in the pan with the foil on it to keep the fish warm while you dress the plates.

4. When the salmon goes into the oven, reheat the curd – be careful not to heat it above 80ºC though as the aga aga will collapse at this heat and become a liquid.

5. Chop the chives and toss them through the leek mix. Season the leeks and beetroot.

6. With a spoon, drag a nice swipe of the curd purée through the middle of each plate. Arrange all of the salad bits to cross over the curd across the length of the plate. Top the salad with tarragon and fennel cress.

7. Remove the salmon from the roasting dish, drain it on kitchen paper and place it next to the salad.

8. Finish the plate with some of the remaining dressing and salmon keta.

"This dish is essentially a cracking piece of fish with a simple salad of complementing flavours and textures."

Pan-fried stone bass with stuffed squid, artichokes & clams

Baby squid makes a perfect little package to stuff with something interesting. In this dish we fill each squid with a pea risotto. The sweet peas and squid work really well together. The rest of the dish is a collection of late spring vegetables which complement the flavours well.

Serves: 6

For the pea risotto:
200g Nage, well-seasoned
(see Basic Recipes)
¼ Small onion
25g Carrot
1 Garlic clove
25g Celery
25g Leek
25g Fennel
17g Vegetable oil
125g Rice
17g Butter
100g Peas
38g White wine
18 Baby squid

1. Bring the nage to a simmer. Cut the vegetables into a neat small dice. Season well with salt and pepper – it is important the stock is properly seasoned as the rice will absorb all the flavour. Imagine you are tasting a soup and season accordingly.

2. In a separate wide pan, heat the vegetable oil, add rice and cook for 1 minute, stirring all the time (it will start to smell nutty). Add the butter, stir in the vegetables and cook for 30 seconds.

3. Add the wine, cook to reduce, then add half the stock and continue cooking. Continue adding the rest of the stock until rice is cooked.

4. Add the peas, check that the rice is cooked through, and pour it onto a flat tray to cool down in the fridge.

5. Wash the squid, chop up the tentacle meat and mix it through the rice mix. Then take each squid tube and half-fill with rice. Reserve in the fridge for later.

36 Clams (6 per person)
6 Spring onions
6 portions of Stone bass
(150-200g each)
Squeeze of lemon juice
Butter
White wine
12 Baby artichokes (prepped
as in Basic Recipes and cut
in quarters lengthways)
100g Samphire, washed
Chives

1. Wash the clams under running cold water for about 1 hour. Discard any that are open or broken.

2. Cut the spring onions to 4cm lengths and cook in well-seasoned water for about 3 minutes, or until tender. Refresh in iced water and pat dry.

3. Season the bass on both sides then fry in a non-stick pan, skin-side down, on a medium heat until skin is crisp. Place some foil over the fish, turn the heat down and continue to cook on the skin side until the fish is cooked through, then remove the pan from the heat.

4. Flip the fish onto the flesh side, add a squeeze of lemon and a knob of butter and allow it to rest in the pan until ready to plate. While the bass is cooking, chargrill the squid in a griddle pan just long enough to see the bar marks.

5. Put a warm sauté pan over a medium heat, add the clams and a glug of white wine. As the wine comes up to the boil add the squid, spring onions and artichokes. Put a lid on and continue to cook for 2 or 3 minutes, or until all the clams are open.

6. Remove from the heat, throw in the samphire and toss.

7. Pass the liquid from the pan into a small saucepan. Over a high heat, reduce it by half.

8. Remove from the heat add a knob of butter and whisk to a good emulsion. Finish the sauce with chopped chives and a drop of fresh lemon juice.

9. Place the fish in the middle of your plates. Arrange the squid tubes and vegetables around the fish and finish with the butter sauce.

Creedy Carver chicken; roast breast & boudin of leg, with Anna potato, girolle mushrooms & broad beans

I really like to use whole chickens – it's more respectful, I feel, and I want customers to enjoy every part of the bird, not just the breasts. The leg meat has by far the most flavour, but the bones seem to upset people, so we take them out for you!

Serves: 4

For the boudin blanc:
275g Pork shoulder
225g Chicken breast
112g Pork fat
2 tsp Salt
2 Pimento
135g Cream
1 Onion
1 tbsp Butter
1 Bay leaf
1½ tsp Black pepper
1 Clove
½ tsp Fresh thyme
¼ tsp Coriander seeds
¼ tsp Caraway seeds
Pinch of cayenne pepper
15g Breadcrumbs

1. This recipe makes far more than is needed, but if you make a smaller amount it gets lost in the mincer. It can be frozen. If this is a lot of bother, then I suggest using a good sausage meat.

2. Put a mixing bowl into freezer. Season the meat and fat with salt and chilli. Soak the breadcrumbs in cream and chill.

3. Finely chop onions, place butter in a frying pan on a low heat and sweat the onions until soft and transparent. Do not brown.

4. Grind all the spices and add to the onion. Chill, then mix with the meats and fat. Mince three times in a food processor/mincer.

5. Put the meat mix into the chilled bowl, add the bread mix and beat with an electric mixer for 5 minutes until light and fluffy. Poach a small amount in a pan of hot water and taste. Adjust the seasoning if required.

1 Creedy Carver free range chicken, approx 1.8kg
Boudin Blanc – see recipe above
Brine (see Basic Recipes)

1. Remove the breasts and legs from the chicken. Cutting along the leg, remove the bones – if you are not sure how to do this, ask the butcher to do it for you.

2. Lay two sheets of foil on your work surface. Season the legs on both sides and place one leg on each piece of foil, skin side down. Spread the leg meat out so that you have two rectangle shapes. Pipe a little of the boudin mix (see recipe below) along the length of each leg. Using the foil, roll up each leg like a cigarette and twist the ends – they should now resemble two Christmas crackers.

3. Poach in simmering water for 2 hours, then refresh in iced water for 1 hour. Chill in the fridge overnight. Brine the chicken breasts for 4 hours. Dry on kitchen paper and store in the fridge.

Creedy Carver chicken; roast breast & boudin of leg, with Anna potato, girolle mushrooms & broad beans (continued)

For the sarladaise potatoes:
1kg Maris Piper potatoes, thinly-sliced and cut into 2.5cm discs
200g Duck fat
Maldon sea salt
5 sprigs fresh Thyme, picked
1 tbsp Roasted garlic pulp
(See Basic recipes)

1. Pre-heat the oven to 180°C.

2. In a straight-sided sauté pan with a metal handle, melt two tablespoons of the duck fat. In a separate pan, mix the rest of the duck fat, garlic and thyme.

3. Arrange a layer of overlapping potatoes all the way around the edge of the saute pan. Season with salt and a dribble of the duck fat and garlic mix. Arrange another layer of potatoes on top. Repeat with the salt and duck fat, then another layer of potato. Repeat until all the potato is used up – the end result should now resemble a tyre.

4. Place the pan on a medium heat and cook until the edges of the potato start to turn a golden brown. Place a foil lid on the pan, and transfer to the oven. Cook for about 40 minutes, or until a small knife passes through the potato with zero resistance. Keep warm before serving.

For the sweetcorn purée:
2 Corn on the cob
100g Chicken stock
100g Whipping cream

1. With a large knife, slice the corn kernels from the cobs. Cook the kernels in the chicken stock and cream, then strain (reserving the liquid).

2. Blend the corn in a food processor, adding some of the liquid in a steady stream until a thick purée consistency is achieved. Be careful not to add too much liquid; you do not want to end up with a soup! Think yoghurt consistency. Adjust the seasoning and then pass through a fine sieve.

For the girolles and broad beans:
250g Girolle mushrooms
250g Broad beans

1. Wash the girolles in warm water and lift out onto a cloth to dry. In the kitchen we use heat lamps, but at home, if it is a sunny day, I put them in the garden in the sun with a clean tea towel over them for a few hours.

2. Boil the broad beans in well-salted water for 2 or 3 minutes until cooked and tender. Refresh into cold water.

3. Pop the beans from their skins.

Other ingredients:

75g Butter
¼ tsp Roasted garlic pulp
(See Basic recipes)
¼ bunch of Marjoram
Madeira sauce (see Basic
Recipes)

To serve:

1. In a heavy-bottomed pan with a metal handle, on a medium heat fry the chicken breast on the skin side. Remove the legs from the foil and place in the pan. Cook, turning the legs so that the skin colours evenly. When the legs and breast skin side is golden and crisp, flip the breast over and add the butter.

2. Cover the chicken with a foil lid. Place in the oven and cook for about 10 minutes. Check the breast is cooked with a thermometer (make sure the centre meat is at 70°C). Allow to rest in the pan.

3. Sauté the girolles in a little butter and the garlic pulp. Add the broad beans. Cook through and season. Finish with some picked marjoram.

4. Drain the mushrooms on some kitchen paper and cut the potato into portion-sized wedges.

5. Slice the chicken breast lengthways, and cut the leg logs into discs 1cm thick.

6. Swipe the sweetcorn purée with a spoon around the edge of the plate, arrange the rest of the ingredients neatly and finish with a little Madeira sauce.

Breast of Creedy Carver duck with Wensleydale spring greens & Black Combe ham, rosemary roast potatoes & fresh fig

Black Combe ham is an air-cured ham produced by Woodhalls in Cumbria. It is utterly delicious. Wensleydale is just the other side of the Pennines, so it seemed a logical cheese to go with the ham.

Serves: 4

4 Creedy Carver duck breasts
400g Spring greens, finely shredded
4 tsp Whipping cream
50g Wensleydale cheese, grated
3 Figs, quartered
8 slices Black Combe ham

For the rosemary potatoes:
2 large Maris Piper potatoes, peeled
1 sprig Rosemary, chopped

For the red wine sauce:
500g Red wine
Zest of 1 orange

1. With a very sharp knife, criss-cross the fat on the duck breasts. Be careful not to go through to the flesh. Season on both sides ready to cook.

2. Prepare the rosemary potatoes. Using a melon baller, scoop out perfectly round potato balls and steam until just cooked.

3. Pre-heat the oven to 180°C. Put the duck in a warm pan, skin down. Keep tipping away the fat which renders out. Don't be tempted to turn the heat up, or speed up this process; you want to achieve a golden brown skin, with nearly all of the fat removed.

4. When ready, cover the pan with a foil lid and cook in the oven for 18 minutes. The duck needs to be cooked just pink, so check the inner meat with a thermometer. It needs to be at 63°C. Remove from the pan and rest for 5 minutes.

5. While the duck is cooking, heat the wine and orange zest. Season the greens and cook in the cream on a gentle heat with the pan lid on. They will take about 4 minutes, but check they are not catching. If they start to look dry, add a tablespoon of water.

6. When cooked, remove the lid and turn the heat up. Stirring constantly, reduce the liquid in the pan until it has nearly all gone. Remove from the heat and beat in the cheese. It should be thick, and not at all wet. Adjust the seasoning.

7. Place the figs in the oven to warm through for 5 minutes.

8. Drop the potato balls in a deep-fat fryer (170°C) and cook until golden. Remove them and roll in the rosemary.

9. Lay two slices of ham along the top of each plate. Arrange the figs and potatoes along the ham and spoon a pile of greens in the middle of each plate. Slice the duck breasts and fan out over the greens.

10. Spoon over the sauce to finish.

Kentish raspberries with cottage cheesecake mille feuille & raspberry sorbet

Raspberries are the last of the berry fruits and are still lovely right through to the beginning of September when everything else has finished. Kent produces some fantastic berry fruit; we get our raspberries from Manor Farm, based just outside of Sevenoaks. The sweet crisp pastry combines so well with the soft sharp raspberries on this dish. The cottage cheese filling should be wonderfully creamy, with just a touch of sweetness from the honey.

Serves: 6

For the cottage cheesecake:
500g Full fat cottage cheese
100g Honey
Zest of 2 lemons

1. Hang the cottage cheese in a muslin cloth in a fridge with a bowl underneath to 'drip dry' for 24 hours.

2. Remove from the fridge and transfer to a bowl with the honey and lemon zest, and gently mix together.

3. Allow to set in the fridge until needed.

For the raspberry sorbet:
700g Raspberries
100g Sugar
100g Double cream
120g Trimoline (can be replaced with glucose)
Lemon juice

1. Blend all of the ingredients in a food processor until smooth, and then pass through a fine sieve to remove all of the raspberry pips. Have a taste and add a few drops of lemon juice if needed.

2. Churn in an ice cream machine and freeze until needed.

For the mille feuille:
200g Puff pastry (see Basic Recipes)
Icing sugar

1. Pre-heat the oven to 160°C.

2. Dust a chopping board with icing sugar and roll out the puff pastry to 2mm thickness. Use more icing sugar as required, or if the pastry sticks – be warned, this job is a bit of a dusty affair!

3. Line a baking sheet with greaseproof paper and dust with icing sugar. Transfer the puff pastry to the baking sheet and dredge the top with more icing sugar. Cover with another sheet of baking paper, and then press down with another baking sheet.

4. Cook for 30 minutes, or until the pastry is golden and crisp. At 160°C, it won't burn very easily, so if you are not sure, give it an extra 10 minutes.

5. When ready, remove from the oven and while still hot, transfer to a cutting board. You need to work quickly now as you need to cut the puff before it cools down, otherwise it will start to shatter.

6. Using a ruler as a guide and a sharp serrated knife, cut the puff pastry into 18 fingers 2cm wide and 10cm long. Any trim that is left can be crushed in a pestle and mortar and reserved for later.

For the raspberry purée:

500g Fresh raspberries
16g Arrowroot
25g Sugar

1. Blend the raspberries in a food processor and pass through a fine sieve.

2. Dissolve the arrowroot in the raspberry juice and cook out on a low heat until nice and thick. Remove from the heat and chill in the fridge.

3. After the purée is well chilled, blend in a food processor until smooth again. Pass through a fine sieve and store in the fridge until required.

Other ingredients:

30 Fresh raspberries
Freeze-dried raspberry powder

To serve:

1. Transfer the cottage cheese to a piping bag fitted with a star nozzle. Lay 12 of the mille feuille fingers on a work surface and pipe the cheese mix along the full length of each finger. Now place one finger on top of the other so that you have six sandwiches of puff/cheese/puff/cheese.

2. Dust the last six fingers that have not yet been used with icing sugar, and place five raspberries on top of each one. Place each raspberry finger on top of the fingers with cottage cheese to complete the mille feuilles.

3. Swipe the raspberry purée across each plate using a warm spoon. Place the mille feuille on one side and a little pile of the reserved puff crumbs on the other. Place a neat scoop of raspberry sorbet on the crumbs.

4. Using a tea strainer lightly dust half of the plate with the freeze-dried raspberries.

*"Raspberries are
the last of the berry
fruits and are still
lovely right through
to the beginning of
September when
everything else has
finished."*

Vanilla cream with fresh Kentish strawberries & warm vanilla doughnuts

Strawberries are available all year now from the supermarkets but they are no longer the treat that they should be, and that is a real shame.

A good old fashioned strawberry like a Royal Sovereign (packed with juiciness and flavour) will not be around for very long in the summer months and so should be eaten and celebrated with much gusto while they are. I often feel that a lot of strawberry puddings have too much going on and are actually trying to disguise the inferiority of medico berries being used. This dessert is as simple as it gets – strawberries, panna cotta cream and warm doughnuts. The latter can be prepared the day before to make things easier.

Serves: 6

For the doughnuts:
125g Flour
16g Sugar
2g Salt
4g Yeast
1 Egg
Zest of ¼ lemon
35g Water
30g Soft butter

1. Using a food mixer on a slow speed, knead the flour, sugar, salt, yeast, egg, lemon zest and water with a dough hook until well incorporated and smooth.

2. Start adding the butter a little at a time, not adding the next piece until the first is incorporated. When all of the butter has been added remove the bowl from the mixer, dust the surface with flour and cover with a kitchen towel.

3. Allow to double in size, then knock back, cover with clingfilm and rest in the fridge overnight.

For the panna cotta cream:
3 leaves Gelatine
500g Crème frâiche
500g Double cream
140g Sugar
2 Vanilla pods

1. Soak the gelatine in cold water.

2. Bring the other ingredients to the boil, then remove from the heat.

3. Squeeze dry the gelatine, add to the cream and whisk in. Pass through a fine sieve and then pour into six glass bowls and refrigerate to set. The amount of gelatine used is very small so that the cream is set… but only just.

Other ingredients:
Royal Sovereign strawberries (lots)
Sugar to roll the doughnuts in

To serve:

1. Wash the strawberries and cut into wedges.

2. Roll the doughnut dough into 20g balls and allow to prove on lightly oiled trays. Dust over with a little flour and loosely cover with clingfilm and rest for 15 minutes or until they double in size.

3. Pile the strawberries onto the panna cotta.

4. Deep-fry the doughnuts at 170°C and constantly flip to give an even golden colour. When cooked, drain on kitchen paper and then roll in caster sugar. Shake off any excess and serve warm with the strawberries and cream.

Apricot-glazed rum baba with orange segments & Cornish clotted cream

Rum baba dough needs to stale slightly before being soaked in the rum syrup. My preference is about one day. If the dough is too fresh the baba will become saturated and soggy (like a biscuit dipped in a cup of tea), too stale and they won't absorb enough syrup and will be hard and dry in the middle. I would recommend making the rum baba the day before.

Serves: 4

For the rum baba:
32g Cream
60g Milk
15g Sugar
15g Yeast
63g Salt
200g Flour
2 Eggs
60g Melted butter

1. Pre-heat the oven to 170ºC.

2. Using a dough hook on a food mixer, knead the cream, milk, sugar, yeast, salt, flour and eggs. Pour the melted butter over the top of the dough without mixing it in and then leave the whole bowl in a warm place to prove and double in size. Now hook back onto the food mixer and knock the dough back by kneading it for a few seconds. This will also incorporate all of the butter.

3. Spoon the dough into baba moulds and fill to two-thirds. Allow to prove again until doubled in size and then cook for 8 minutes (turning after 5 minutes in the oven).

4. Once cool, store the babas in an air-tight box until needed.

For the syrup:
750g Sugar
1kg Water
1 Cinnamon stick
1 Vanilla pod
Zest of 1 Lemon
Zest of 1 Orange
100g Rum

1. Bring all of the ingredients to the boil, then remove from the heat.

2. Using a thermometer, let the syrup cool to 30ºC then add the baba, basting them in the warm syrup as they bob about.

3. After about 2 minutes, gently lift the baba onto a wire rack and allow them to rest upside down.

For the apricot and rum glaze:
200g Apricot jam
20g Dark rum

1. Whilst the babas are draining, over a medium heat whisk the jam and the rum together. As it comes to the boil, remove from the heat and pass through a fine sieve.

2. Turn the babas the correct way up and using a pastry brush, liberally apply the glaze all over.

Other ingredients:
60 Orange segments
Cornish clotted cream
30 sprigs of Mint

To serve:

1. Place a baba in the centre of each plate and fan the orange segments around. Using a warm ice cream scoop, drop a ball of clotted cream on top of each baba and finish with fresh mint sprigs.

September October November

Home-cured salmon with beetroot, crème frâiche & dill

Cornish mackerel, chicory & grilled potato salad

Ravioli of Wiltshire truffle & chestnut with shaved truffle

Butternut soup with sage pesto, toasted pumpkin seeds
& toasted crusts

Warm salad of wood pigeon & baked autumn vegetables,
port dressing and chestnuts

Roast haunch of venison with venison dumplings, crushed
swede, cabbage & bacon

Colne Valley lamb; roast loin & glazed shoulder with fried
polenta, Jerusalem artichoke and buttered kale

Courgette & broccoli lasagna with courgette fritter,
red peppers, balsamic & pesto dressing

Roasted Jerusalem artichokes, scorched onions & grilled
leeks, with hazelnut & caper scones and red wine

Chocolate ale cake with white chocolate mousse,
honeycomb & ginger ice cream

Blackberry soufflé and fresh blackberries with vanilla
custard & apple crumble ice cream

Home-cured salmon with beetroot, crème frâiche & dill

This recipe is similar to the Scandinavian Gravlax. It seems like a lot of salt, but don't worry, the salt is to draw the water out of the fish to intensify the flavour. One side of salmon is the minimum amount of fish I would cure as small portions will over-cure. This dish makes a fantastic buffet starter, as it is so simple, and all of the work is done the day before. If I serve this at home (and I have done) I just slice the salmon and arrange it over a chopping board for guests to help themselves with a large bowl of the crème frâiche.

Serves: 10

To cure the salmon:
10g Coriander seeds
8g Cloves
2 Star anise
2 bunch Dill
500g Salt
420g Sugar
Zest and juice of 1 lemon
Zest and juice of 1 lime
10g White pepper
1 fillet Salmon

1. Grind the spices and roughly chop the dill. Mix all of the ingredients (except the salmon) in a large bowl.

2. In a large container (the length of the fish) sprinkle half of the salt cure and place the salmon on top. Cover the salmon with the rest of the salt mix. Cover the container with clingfilm and refrigerate. Every six hours, remove the fish, turn it over and put it back in the container and cover back over with the salt. During the curing process, lots of water will be drawn out of the salmon; this is normal and by the time it has had 24 hours your piece of fish will almost be swimming in the container.

3. After 24 hours remove the fish from the cure and wrap up in a clean tea towel and return to the fridge for a couple of hours. The tea towel will absorb any remaining salty liquid on the fish. It seems a bit of a waste, but the cure is finished now and can be thrown away.

For the beetroot:
1kg Beetroot
200g Red wine vinegar
20g Sugar
30g Salt

1. Peel the beetroot and using a turning mandolin, cut the beetroot into long 'spaghetti'.

2. Transfer to a large bowl, add the vinegar, sugar, salt and mix well. Store the beetroot in the fridge overnight.

3. The following day, pour the beetroot into a colander to drain off the liquid that will have been released. Taste some, and if required, add a little more seasoning.

For the crème fraîche:
1kg Crème fraîche
Salt and pepper
Lemon
½ bunch Dill

1. Hang the crème fraîche in a muslin cloth over a bowl in the fridge overnight to allow all of the excess liquid to drip out. After 24 hours the crème fraîche will be much thicker.

2. Transfer to a clean bowl and season with freshly milled salt and pepper (don't be shy with the pepper) and a few drops of lemon juice.

3. Pick the dill leaves from the stalks, chop nice and fine and then fold into the crème fraîche. Check the seasoning and store until ready to serve.

To serve:

1. Using an extremely sharp knife, using long slow strokes, slice the salmon as thin as you can – it takes a bit of practice. Have a nibble on any slices that look too thick.

2. Swirl the beetroot strands around a carving fork to form neat little nests and place onto each plate. Using a warm spoon, neatly scoop the crème fraîche on to the plates and finish with the slices of salmon.

Cornish mackerel, chicory & grilled potato salad

In my mind, mackerel is great any time of year, it has so much flavour and is so versatile – grill it, smoke it, make a pâté. We should be eating more mackerel as it is very healthy too. This dish is all about the dressing, so that the big flavours of the fish and the slight bitterness of the leaves are balanced out and everything works together.

Serves: 6

For the salad and dressing:
3 heads Endive
2 Pears
1 Red onion
40g Golden raisins
10g Grain mustard
15g Chardonnay vinegar
90g Extra virgin olive oil
Zest and juice of 1 orange
Maldon sea salt

1. Cut the bottom root from the endive and carefully separate the leaves. Wash well.

2. Using a 5mm melon baller (yes, they do exist that small) take tiny little balls out of the pears and add to a large bowl. Peel the red onion and cut to the thinnest slice you can. Add the sliced onion to the pear balls followed by the raisins, mustard, vinegar and olive oil.

3. On a micro plane, zest the orange into the bowl and then squeeze in the juice. Gently mix the ingredients and allow to rest for 30 minutes to let the flavours develop a little. Adjust the seasoning with a little salt if required.

For the potatoes:
12 New potatoes
50g Extra virgin olive oil

1. Peel the potatoes and slice to about 5mm. Cook in a steamer (steaming them prevents them from becoming waterlogged).

2. Whilst they are still warm toss in the olive oil.

For the mackerel:
6 Mackerel fillets (skin on)
½ bunch Flat leaf parsley
½ bunch picked Dill

1. Pre-heat a chargrill.

2. Slice the herbs and toss them with the endive leaves. Now add the dressing a little at a time. You don't want to saturate the leaves but they should take most of the dressing.

3. Arrange the warm potatoes and the salad on plates.

4. Brush the mackerel with a little vegetable oil and season with table salt.

5. Grill the fish on the skin side and allow it to char until the flesh side starts to feel warm to the touch. The fish will grill very quickly so make sure you have everything else finished before you start cooking. Carefully remove the fish and flake over your salad.

Ravioli of Wiltshire truffle & chestnut with shaved truffle

I use English truffles at the restaurant from their secret location in Wiltshire. Truffles are an ingredient that have a lot of mystery and myth about them and should be a real treat to be enjoyed when they are in season. The fact that we can now get truffles in this country is brilliant, and usually causes a bit of surprise from customers. The Wiltshire truffles are not as strong as the Perigord truffles from France or the Alba white truffles of Italy, but they are a real treat nonetheless. Needless to say, truffles are expensive, so don't waste anything when making this dish.

Serves: 6

Pasta dough (see Basic Recipes)
100g Wiltshire truffles

1. Roll out the pasta as described in the Basic Recipes section and roll it down to number 3 on the pasta machine.

2. Using a 50mm cutter, cut out 12 pasta discs and cover with a damp cloth to stop them drying out.

3. Clean the truffles with a small brush – a soft new toothbrush is ideal for this – and then peel off the outer crust, keeping all of the peelings. The truffles are now ready to use later.

For the sauce:
1kg Double cream
Truffle peelings from above
Ximenez sherry vinegar
Salt

1. Using a sharp knife, chop the truffle trimmings as fine as possible.

2. In a heavy pan, bring the cream to the boil and reduce to about a third of its original volume. When reduced, remove the cream from the heat and add the chopped truffle peelings, only a couple of drops of the sherry vinegar and a pinch of salt. Pop a lid on the pan and allow to rest for 10 minutes whilst you prepare the ravioli.

For the potato filling:
600g Baking potatoes
100g Cooked chestnuts
100g Sauce (from above)

1. Wash the potatoes and bake in the oven as you would for a jacket potato. When cooked and still hot, cut the potatoes in half and scoop the filling out from the skin.

2. Discard the skin and pass the filling though a potato masher, with the chestnuts, into a large bowl. Season the potatoes and add 100g of the truffle sauce. Add a little seasoning and mix well together. Transfer the mix into a piping bag.

Other ingredients:

Raw couscous

To serve:

1. Tip the couscous onto a large flat tray.

2. Run one of the pasta discs through the pasta machine on number 1 and lay it on a well floured work surface. Repeat, so that you now have two thin discs of pasta.

3. Pipe a sixth of the filling into the centre of one of the pasta discs, making sure to leave a clear edge around the filling so that the pasta can be crimped together. Place the second disc on top and crimp the two pieces of pasta together all of the way around. Using a 90mm fluted cutter, trim off any excess pasta.

4. Rest the ravioli on the couscous to prevent it sticking to your work surface. Now repeat the whole process until all six raviolis are complete.

5. Bring a large pan of water to the boil and the sauce back to the simmer.

6. Cook the pasta in the water until they float. Using a slotted spoon remove from the water and drain on kitchen towel.

7. Transfer each pasta to a warm plate and drizzle over the sauce. Finish by shaving the fresh truffle over each plate until there is none left.

Butternut soup with sage pesto, toasted pumpkin seeds & toasted crusts

A British Autumn menu has to feature butternut squash soup, doesn't it? A soup can be a thing of great delight if made with care and attention, or (as is usually the case) a warm, wet puddle of something that used to have flavour. The secret to any soup is to not overcook it. Soups want to be fresh and vibrant and not taste 'stewed', especially if they are vegetable based. We roast the butternut squash for this soup, as the light caramelisation intensifies the flavour.

Serves: 4

For the butternut soup:
2 Butternut squash
3 Shallots
Olive oil
500g Nage (see Basic Recipes)
500g Cream
500g Milk
125g Butter
Nutmeg, to taste

1. Pre-heat the oven to 170°C with a roasting tray inside.

2. Peel the butternut squash and cut them in half lengthways and scoop out the seeds. Cut the squash into large chunks. Cut the shallots in half and toss the two together in a large bowl with a splash of olive oil to just coat.

3. Transfer the mixture to the roasting tray in the oven and cook for about 30 minutes or until the flesh is soft and golden brown.

4. Whilst the squash is baking in the oven, in a heavy-based pan bring the nage, cream and milk to the boil. When it boils, add the cooked butternut squash. Bring back to the boil and remove from the heat.

5. Allow to cool slightly before blending in a food processor with the butter. Adjust the seasoning and rasp in a little nutmeg to taste. Pass the soup through a fine sieve.

For the pesto of pumpkin seed and marjoram:
40g Pumpkin seeds
Olive oil, to roast
40g Marjoram
40g Parsley
1 tsp Roasted garlic pulp
(see Basic Recipes)
80g Extra virgin olive oil
40g Old Winchester cheese, finely grated

1. Toast the pumpkin seeds in the oven with a little olive oil at the same time as you cook the butternut squash.

2. Blend the toasted pumpkin seeds, marjoram, parsley, roasted garlic pulp and extra virgin olive oil in a food processor. Add the Old Winchester cheese and fold in by hand.

For the toasted crusts:
2 slices of bread
Olive oil

1. Cut the slices of bread about 5mm thick from a loaf of bread. Further cut those slices into 5mm cubes. Toss the bread in olive oil and toast in the oven on a baking sheet as the butternut squash is cooking. Cook until golden and crisp.

To serve:

1. Pour the soup into a warm bowl, sprinkle over the crusts and spoon over some of the pesto.

Warm salad of wood pigeon & baked autumn vegetables, port dressing and chestnuts

Pigeon is such an autumnal ingredient in my mind. Cooked pink its meat is very tender, with a distinct rich flavour. Because they are only small birds, pigeon make for a wonderful starter and can stand up to the bold flavours of the root vegetables that are in season. I am not too keen on hot and cold food on the same dish, so we make all of the salad ingredients warm, it is more comforting to eat then too.

Serves: 6

For the Cumberland dressing:

2 Red onions
150g Port
12g Cabernet sauvignon red wine vinegar
Juice and zest of 2 oranges
150g Redcurrant jelly
30g Hazelnut oil

1. Peel and dice the onions very finely and add to a pan with the port and the vinegar. Over a gentle heat, reduce the port mix by three-quarters – it should start to thicken up and turn syrupy.

2. Add orange juice, zest and redcurrant jelly and bring back to the boil. Remove from the heat, mix in the hazelnut oil and keep warm until needed.

For the vegetables:

6 Heritage beetroots of different colours (see Basic Recipes)
½ Celeriac
Chilli flakes
6 sticks Salsify
Olive oil
Lemon juice

1. Pre-heat the oven to 200ºC.

2. Slice the beetroots to 5mm thickness and reserve for later.

3. Peel the outer skin from the celeriac and rub all over with olive oil, seasoning and chilli flakes. Wrap the whole thing in foil and bake in the oven until tender to the spike of a knife, approximately 25 minutes.

4. Allow the celeriac to cool slightly and then slice into matchsticks. Reserve for later.

5. Peel the salsify and roast half of it in the oven with the celeriac for about 12 minutes or until just tender. Allow to cool then slice into 4cm batons.

6. Keep all of the vegetables warm.

7. Using a vegetable peeler slice ribbons off the remaining three salsify and store in a container with cold water and a squeeze of fresh lemon juice to stop it from going brown.

For the wood pigeon:

6 Skinless pigeon breasts

Other ingredients:

Chestnuts
Mustard frills
Celery cress

1. Two hours before cooking, remove the pigeon breasts from the fridge to allow them to come up to room temperature.

2. Pre-heat a chargrill.

3. Season the pigeon. Brush over a little vegetable oil then cook on the chargrill. Pigeon needs to be served very pink otherwise it will be tough and chewy. The best way to cook it is to turn it every 30 seconds and only cook the breasts for a total of 90 seconds.

4. Remove the breasts from the grill and place them on a warm plate. Cover the plate with foil and let the meat rest for 2 minutes. I take the internal temperature of pigeon to 59ºC. Slice each breast into six.

To serve:

1. In the centre of each plate lay four or five slices of beetroot and scatter around some of the celeriac, roast salsify and salsify ribbons.

2. Arrange the pigeon slices on the plate and drizzle over some of the warm dressing.

3. Finish the plate with plenty of shaved chestnuts, mustard frills and celery cress.

Roast haunch of venison with venison dumplings, crushed swede, cabbage & bacon

A whole venison leg has different cuts on it that need to be treated and cooked differently. The top of the leg (thigh) is very lean and when trimmed properly is juicy and tender cooked pink. On the lower leg the shin is very tough and needs a long slow cook to tenderise it, but it is full of flavour. Eating both cuts together you can enjoy a lovely contrast of braised versus roast.

Serves: 10

For the venison:
4kg Venison leg on the bone
3 bottles red wine
½ bunch thyme
2 bay leaves
100g Carrots
100g Onions
100g Mushrooms
100g Smoked bacon
4kg Veal stock
Red wine vinegar

Two days before:

1. Remove the venison meat from the bone and then remove the shin from the thigh – you can ask a butcher to do this for you.

2. Pour two bottles of red wine into a container and add the shin meat with the thyme and bay leaves. Marinate in the fridge for 24 hours.

3. Running through the thigh muscles there are some fairly large sinews that need to be removed by running a very sharp knife along both sides. The sinews are easy to spot and form the boundary between each muscle in the thigh, so when they are removed you will have actually separated the constituent muscles of the thigh and should be left with three large chunks of clean meat – again, if you have not done this before, ask for a butcher's assistance. Wrap the venison meat in clingfilm and refrigerate until required.

4. All of the trim can be reserved for the sauce.

The day before:

1. Pre-heat the oven to 120°C.

2. Remove the venison shin from the marinade, pat dry on a tea towel and discard the wine. Season the shin meat all over with table salt and rest for 30 minutes.

3. After the meat has rested wipe it clean with kitchen towel. In a wide shallow pan, or roasting dish with a good lug of vegetable oil, on a high heat fry the shin meat until it is caramelised all over – it should be a deep mahogany colour. Transfer the meat to a deep casserole dish and now (in the same pan) fry the carrots, onion, mushrooms and smoked bacon. When golden, tip all of the contents of the pan through a colander sat over a bowl. The fat collected in the bowl can be discarded, and the vegetables and bacon added to the casserole dish.

4. Deglaze the original pan with the last bottle of red wine and reduce by half, then pour the contents into the casserole. Add the veal stock into the casserole to just cover the contents.

5. On a medium heat bring the contents of the casserole to the simmer and then put the lid on and transfer to the oven. Cook the casserole until the meat is very tender – approximately 4 hours.

6. When cooked, remove the lid and let the casserole cool down for 1 hour. Gently lift the meat from the pot and transfer it to a tray. Pass the liquid through a colander into a clean pan – discard the vegetables and bacon, they will have imparted all of their flavour.

7. Over a medium heat reduce the venison liquid until it is thick and sticky.

8. Whilst the stock is reducing, shred the venison meat and pick out any gristle.

9. Once the stock has reduced, mix it with the shredded meat, a few drops of red wine vinegar and any seasoning if it is required. Portion the meat into 60g balls and chill in the fridge.

10. The rest of the elements can be prepared on the day.

For the dumplings:
200g Self-raising flour
70g Suet
4g Salt
Pinch of dried Thyme
85g Milk
140g Chicken livers
1kg chicken stock

1. In a food processor, blend the flour, suet, salt and dried thyme to 'breadcrumbs' texture. Add the milk and the chicken livers and blend to just incorporate. Ball the dough into 50g balls and rest in the fridge for 30 minutes.

2. Using well-floured fingers, pinch the dough balls into flat discs, and wrap them around the venison balls to form a dumpling.

For the crushed swede:
4 Swedes
Salt and pepper
200g Unsalted butter
100g Water

1. Peel and dice the swede into uniform chunks and place into a pan with some seasoning, butter and half of the water. On a low heat with the lid on, cook the swede until soft. Add the rest of the water as required during the cooking process to ensure that the swede cooks in an emulsion of the butter and the water.

2. When cooked, mill in plenty of black pepper and 'pulse' blend on a food processor to lightly crush the swede.

For the cabbage:
1 Savoy cabbage

1. Remove the stem from each leaf of cabbage and finely shred the leaves.

Roast haunch of venison with venison dumplings, crushed swede, cabbage & bacon (continued)

Other ingredients:

Venison sauce (see Basic Recipes)
Sage
Bacon
Cauliflower purée (see Basic Recipes)

1. Pre-heat the oven to 180°C.

2. Remove the venison leg from the fridge and season all over 2 hours before cooking.

3. In a heavy-based pan, on a high heat roast off the three venison leg loins and then transfer from the pan to a roasting rack. Cook in the oven until the internal temperature reaches 50°C.

4. Remove from the oven and lightly cover with foil to rest – during resting the venison should reach 56-60°C and be lovely and pink.

5. To cook the dumplings, bring the stock to the boil and pour it into a baking dish. Add the dumplings and cook in the oven for 12 minutes. Remove from the oven and cover with foil.

6. In separate pans, heat the cauliflower purée, crushed swede and the venison sauce (adding fresh slices of sage).

7. In a large saucepan, with a little butter and a splash of water, steam the cabbage with a lid on.

To serve:

1. Carve the venison leg and rest on kitchen towel. Season well with Maldon sea salt and pepper.

2. Swipe cauliflower purée through the centre of each plate. Quenelle the crushed swede between two spoons, place it next to the cauliflower.

3. Make a little pile of cabbage, and place a dumpling on top.

4. Finally arrange some sliced meat on the plate and sauce over.

Colne Valley lamb; roast loin & glazed shoulder with fried polenta, Jerusalem artichoke and buttered kale

Loin of lamb, or the cannon as it is sometimes called, has all of the fat and skin removed and is a lovely lean cut of meat. Cooked pink it is utterly delicious.

Serves: 8

For the glazed lamb shoulder:
2kg Lamb shoulder on the bone
Roasted garlic pulp (see Basic Recipes)
Maldon sea salt
4 sprigs Rosemary, chopped
500g Chicken stock
250g Caramelised onions (see Basic Recipes)

1. Prepare the glazed shoulder the day before serving.

2. Pre-heat the oven to 175ºC.

3. Score the skin and fat of the lamb with a sharp knife and then rub all over with roasted garlic pulp, salt and picked, chopped rosemary, and allow to rest for 30 minutes.

4. On a roasting rack cook the lamb for about 30 minutes, or until the skin is golden all over and fat is oozing out of the score marks.

5. Turn the oven down to 150ºC. Transfer the shoulder to a large casserole dish and add the chicken stock. Bring the stock to the simmer, pop on the lid and bake in the oven until the meat is falling from the bone.

6. When cooked, allow the lamb to cool for 30 minutes before removing it from the casserole. Pass the cooking liquid into a clean saucepan and reduce by half. Store in the fridge until needed.

7. Pick the lamb from the bone and discard any gristle. Mix the picked lamb with the caramelised onions and adjust the seasoning. Lay a double sheet of clingfilm on a work surface and, working on the clingfilm, shape the lamb mix into a sausage shape about 3cm in diameter. Roll up the sausage in the clingfilm and tie the ends.

For the polenta:
1kg Milk
125g Butter
250g Chicken stock
250g Polenta
50g Old Winchester cheese, grated
Seasoning, to taste

1. Boil the milk, butter and chicken stock in a large pan. Add the polenta and whisk. When thick and cooked, add the cheese and seasoning.

2. Line a 30cm brownie tin with baking paper and fill with the polenta. Using a spatula smooth off the top and then chill to set.

Colne Valley lamb; roast loin & glazed shoulder with fried polenta, Jerusalem artichoke and buttered kale (continued)

For the lamb loins:

4 Loins of lamb (about 400g each)
Vegetable oil, for roasting
100g Butter, for roasting
2 sprigs Rosemary
1 Garlic clove

Other ingredients:

500g Curly kale, stalks removed
550g Lamb sauce (see Basic Recipes)
Jerusalem artichoke purée (see Basic Recipes)
24 Roast baby onions

1. Pre-heat the oven to 160°C.

2. Heat a deep-fat fryer to 170°C.

3. Remove the log of lamb shoulder from the fridge and cut it into eight portions of about 7g each, and then remove the clingfilm. In a non-stick pan, gently fry the shoulder logs on one end until lightly caramelised. Flip over and caramelise the other end (this light crust will stop the shoulder logs falling apart when they are glazed in the oven). Tip the oil from the pan and then add the reserved cooking liquid. Bring to the boil and place in the oven. Baste over the juices every 5 minutes to achieve a nice glaze.

4. Remove the polenta from the brownie tin and cut into eight rectangles. Cut the rectangles in half corner to corner so that you are left with 16 triangles.

5. Season the lamb loins with salt and pepper and fry in a little oil on all sides. Reduce the heat and add the butter, a sprig of rosemary and a crushed garlic clove. Continue cooking in the pan, turning the meat every minute, frequently basting over the butter. This is a lovely way to cook smaller pieces of meat. The butter should stay a lovely golden brown. If it starts to darken then the pan is too hot and the heat needs to be reduced. Cook the loins to an internal temperature of 60°C and allow to rest for 5 minutes before serving.

6. Deep-fry the polenta until golden.

7. In a large saucepan with a little butter and a splash of water, steam the curly kale with a lid on. Heat the Jerusalem artichoke purée and the lamb sauce.

To serve:

1. Make two swipes of Jerusalem artichoke purée across the top and bottom of the plates in opposite directions – almost like a train track of purée across each plate. Place the glazed lamb shoulder at one end and a little pile of kale at the other. Slice the loins and arrange on the kale. Finish with the polenta, baby onions and sauce.

Courgette & broccoli lasagna with courgette fritter, red peppers, balsamic & pesto dressing

We always get a lot of compliments for this dish. Courgette and broccoli does not sound that exciting but with the spice of the fritter, the sweetness of the pepper and the basil and cheese in the filling, I think it is pleasantly more flavoursome than perhaps anticipated.

Serves: 8

For the pepper purée:
8 Red peppers
20g Extra virgin olive oil

1. Pre-heat the grill.

2. Grill the peppers until black and blistered all over and completely collapsed, approximately 7 minutes. Transfer the peppers to a bowl and cover in clingfilm to rest.

3. After 10 minutes remove the seeds and burnt skin from the peppers. Blend the liquid that has been released with the peppers, olive oil and a little seasoning until smooth. Pass through a fine sieve into a clean pan. Reserve.

For the courgette fritter:
350g Courgettes
Table salt
5g Cumin seeds
5g Coriander seeds
1 Fresh chilli
1 Garlic clove
5g Root ginger
110g Gram flour
10g Greek yoghurt
2g Turmeric
2 Small onions, very fine slice
½ tsp Garam masala
¼ bunch Mint, fine chiffonade

1. Grate the courgettes on a coarse grate and season with table salt. After 20 minutes, using a clean tea towel, squeeze the courgettes dry – the salt will have expelled a lot of liquid from the courgettes. You need 225g of drained courgette.

2. Mix all of the ingredients together in a large bowl and adjust the seasoning – it should be a very thick paste.

3. Reserve for later.

For the white sauce:
43g Butter
65g Onion, diced
50g Flour
250g Milk
250g Whipping cream
125g Nage (see Basic Recipes)
1 Bay leaf
3 Peppercorns
3 Cloves
120g Old Winchester cheese

1. Melt the butter in a suitable pan. Add the onion and cook until soft – no colour.

2. Add the flour and cook out for 5 minutes. Add the milk, cream, nage, bay leaf, peppercorns and cloves and whisk to the boil. Reduce the heat to very low, put a lid on the pan and cook out for 40 minutes, whisking occasionally.

3. Pass through a fine sieve into a clean pan and fold in the cheese.

Courgette & broccoli lasagna with courgette fritter, red peppers, balsamic & pesto dressing (continued)

For the broccoli and courgette lasagna:

720g Courgette, cut in to ribbons on mandolin
900g Broccoli
100g Old Winchester cheese, grated
90g Pine nuts
90g Walnuts
20g Pesto
Pasta dough (see Basic Recipes)

1. In a steaming pan, cook the vegetables for 2 minutes and allow to cool on a tray. Transfer to a large bowl and mix in the cheese, pesto and nuts and bind with a little of the white sauce.

2. Roll out the pasta as described in the Basic Recipes section to number 2 on a machine.

3. In a pan of boiling, salted water cook the pasta sheet until just done and then, using a slotted spoon, transfer the pasta to a pan of iced water.

4. Once cool, remove the cooked pasta sheet from the water and lay out along a work surface. Rub a little olive oil into the pasta – this will stop it sticking. Using a 90mm cutter cut out 24 discs. Store them until needed.

To serve:

1. Using two spoons, quenelle eight courgette fritters and deep-fry them (170°C).

2. In separate pans, warm the pepper purée, white sauce and the lasagna filling.

3. Place a 90mm ring on each plate and put a pasta disc flat on the plate. Spoon in some of the filling to half fill the ring and then add another pasta disc. Spoon in more filling to the top of the ring and finish with a pasta disc.

4. Draw a couple of swipes of pepper purée on each plate and a place a fritter on the purée. Remove the metal rings and finish with white sauce.

Roasted Jerusalem artichokes, scorched onions & grilled leeks, with hazelnut & caper scones and red wine

I love Jerusalem artichokes, we use them a lot and they have such a distinctive nutty flavour. You must cook Jerusalems with care though, as if you overcook them they will just turn to mush. When I was learning to cook, we used to cook artichokes in acidulated water, but I much prefer to bake them now.

Serves: 6

For the vegetables:
300g Jerusalem artichokes
Olive oil
Salt and pepper, to season
3 Leeks
9 Small English onions

1. Pre-heat the oven to 200ºC.

2. Peel the artichokes and toss in a little olive oil and seasoning.

3. Trim the green and the root from the leeks and wash well. In a steamer pan cook the leeks until tender. Allow the leeks to cool, and cut in half lengthways, then cut each half equally into three.

4. With the skin still intact and cutting from the top, cut the onions into eight wedges, but don't cut all the way through. Stop just above the root of the onion so that they stay intact. Brush with a little olive oil and a twist of salt. Bake in the oven until the onion is tender. The outside will start to char (giving a lovely bittersweet taste to the finished onions).

5. Remove the onions from the oven and fully separate the scorched segments. Discard the skin, and arrange the onion segments on the baking sheet with the scones.

For the caper and parsley scones:
350g Self-raising flour
50g Butter, diced
50g Hazelnut oil
50g Capers
10g Curly parsley
70g Yoghurt
35g Water
Salt

1. In a food mixer, using the 'K' beater on the slowest speed, crumb the flour, diced butter and hazelnut oil. Add the capers, chopped parsley, yoghurt and water and bring to a ball. Wrap in clingfilm and rest in the fridge.

2. On a lightly floured work surface, roll out the scone mix to about 15mm thickness. Cut out using a 25mm cutter. Place the scones onto a baking sheet and brush with egg wash and some freshly milled sea salt.

For the red wine glaze:
1 bottle red wine
½ bottle Port
Cabernet sauvignon red wine vinegar

1. In a wide pan reduce the port and red wine by three-quarters to a sticky glaze. Add a few drops of red wine vinegar. Transfer to a bottle and reserve for later.

Other ingredients:
Cooked chestnuts
Purple broccoli shoots
Curly kale
Jerusalem artichoke purée
(see Basic Recipes)

1. Warm the artichoke purée.

2. On a chargrill, grill the leeks cut face side down.

3. Add the artichokes to a hot roasting tray and cook in the oven. The baking sheet with scones and onion wedges can go into the oven at the same time. The scones will take 6 minutes to cook. In this time the onions will get good and hot.

4. In a pan of salted water, cook the broccoli and the kale. Drain off and lightly season.

To serve:

1. Arrange and scatter all of the ingredients over the plates. Finish with a drizzle of the reduced red wine and plenty of shaved chestnuts.

Chocolate ale cake with white chocolate mousse, honeycomb & ginger ice cream

Ale and chocolate are wonderful partners. The ale really enhances the chocolate notes, whilst keeping the sponge nice and moist. This dish is a bit seventies with the brandy snaps and honeycomb, but made well, all of the textures and flavours work well together.

Serves: 8

For the brandy snap:
75g Butter
50g Sugar
50g Golden syrup
50g Flour
1g Ginger powder
Zest of ½ an orange
1 tsp Brandy

You will need:
15mm Doweling wood

1. Pre-heat the oven to 180°C.

2. Cream the butter, sugar and golden syrup in a mixing bowl. Add the flour, ginger, finely grated orange zest and the brandy. Mix well and rest for 30 minutes in the fridge.

3. Line a baking sheet with a silicone mat. Pull off 12g balls from the dough and flatten with the palm of your hand onto the silicone mat. When cooking, the dough will spread out to about 10cm in diameter, so make sure you leave plenty of room between them.

3. Bake in the oven for about 7 minutes or until golden. Remove the tray from the oven and allow to cool just long enough for the brandy snaps to become pliable. At this point, working very quickly, before the brandy snaps set and turn brittle, roll one of the snaps around the doweling – it will set very quickly. Once it does, slide out the wood and repeat for the next one. If the snaps set before you have had chance to roll them all, slide them back in the oven for a moment to re-melt them and continue. You need eight brandy snap 'tubes'.

For the honeycomb:
300g Sugar
200g Golden syrup
8g White wine vinegar
150g Water
2 tsp Bicarbonate of soda

1. Line a 20cm baking tray with greaseproof paper.

2. Add the sugar, golden syrup, white wine vinegar and water to a heavy-based pan and bring to the boil. Using a sugar thermometer, boil the syrup until it reaches 165°C.

3. As soon as it reaches temperature, remove from the heat and whisk in the bicarbonate soda. Pour into the baking tin and leave at room temperature to set. When set, shatter the honeycomb with a whack from a rolling pin.

Chocolate ale cake with white chocolate mousse, honeycomb & ginger ice cream (continued)

For the ale chocolate cake:
110g Butter
175g Dark brown sugar
2 Eggs
100g Self-raising flour
60g Ground almonds
175g Sam Smiths ale
50g Cocoa powder
75g Chocolate buttons (70%)

1. Pre-heat the oven to 160°C.

2. Cream the butter and brown sugar and then add the eggs, one at a time, making sure that the last is fully incorporated before adding the next. Fold in the flour and the almonds, and finally fold in the ale, cocoa and chocolate.

3. Pour into a 1kg 'V'-shaped cake tin and cook for 15-20 minutes or until an inserted skewer comes out clean. Turn out of the cake tin and rest on a wire rack sat over a shallow tray.

For the chocolate glaze:
1 leaf Gelatine
200g Water
125g Sugar
40g Cocoa
120g Chocolate buttons (70%)
50g White chocolate

1. Soften the gelatine in cold water.

2. Melt the water, sugar and cocoa in a pan and bring to the simmer. Remove from the heat and add the chocolate buttons and the gelatine.

3. Whisk smooth and then pass through a fine sieve. Allow to cool at room temperature for 30 minutes before use.

4. When the cake has cooled for an hour, spoon the cool glaze over the top. Allow to set for 20 minutes and then give the cake a second coat of the glaze. Allow to set.

5. Add the white chocolate to a small piping bag and melt it on the defrost setting in a microwave. When melted, drizzle the white chocolate over the cake to decorate.

For the ginger ice cream:
500g Milk
500g Double cream
250g Glucose
80g Trimoline
Zest of 2 oranges
5cm Fresh ginger, grated
8 Egg yolks
200g Sugar

1. Bring the milk, double cream, glucose, trimoline, orange zest and ginger to the boil.

2. Now follow the method for vanilla ice cream basic recipe (see page 187).

Other ingredients
8 x Tuile baskets (see Basic Recipes)
½ recipe White chocolate mousse (see Basic Recipes)

To serve:

1. Slice the cake into eight portions.

2. Fill a piping bag with the white chocolate mousse and pipe it into the brandy snaps.

3. Scatter honeycomb over the plates. Place a slice of cake at one end and a tuile basket at the other. Fill the tuile basket with ginger ice cream. Rest a brandy snap on to the ice cream.

Blackberry soufflé and fresh blackberries with vanilla custard & apple crumble ice cream

I have included this recipe because it is utterly delicious, and seasonal, but I have to confess, it is also a bit of a cheat. We struggled for a long time in the kitchen to use fresh blackberries to flavour the soufflé. We made different jams, purées and syrups, but could not get anything to work without destabilising the soufflé and ending up with pancakes. In the end, I resorted to a bought in purée. I don't know why, but the Boiron purée works perfectly – at least I'm honest about it!

Serves: 8

For the rice pudding:
1 Vanilla pod
300g Milk
250g (+ 150g) Cream
Pinch salt
90g Sugar
120g Rice
350g Blackberry Boiron purée

1. Pre-heat the oven to 120°C.

2. Cut the vanilla pod in half and scrape out the seeds. Mix with all of the other ingredients and add to a large pan. Bring to the simmer, stirring all the time. Put a lid on the pan, and bake in the oven for about 1 hour.

3. Remove from the oven and add the extra cream.

4. Blend in a food processor until smooth. Pass through a fine sieve and cool.

For the soufflé (makes 8 medium pudding moulds):
160g Rice pudding (see above)
160g Blackberry Boiron purée
4 Eggs (separated)
60g Sugar

1. Pre-heat the oven to 180°C.

2. Line eight 250ml pudding moulds with butter, and then sugar.

3. In a large bowl, over simmering water, cook the rice pudding, blackberry purée and egg yolks until they start to thicken. This will only take about 5 minutes, but you do need to whisk all the time. Keep the hot water for later. Remove from the heat.

4. Whisk the egg whites and the sugar to a glossy meringue then fold into the rice pudding mix in three batches – you will find the whites incorporate much easier if you are quite vigorous with the first inclusion. Make sure that the mix is completely homogeneous before adding the next two batches of egg whites.

5. Distribute the soufflé mix carefully between the eight moulds. Place the moulds into an oven dish and then fill the dish with boiling water to come half way up the moulds. Bake for 8 minutes until well risen and golden, and then remove the baking dish from the oven, and allow the soufflés to cool in the water for 10 minutes.

6. After the rest, turn the soufflés out onto greaseproof paper and store in the fridge until ready to serve. The soufflés will keep for about 12 hours in the fridge, after this they will not rise so well when cooked.

Blackberry soufflé and fresh blackberries with vanilla custard & apple crumble ice cream (continued)

For the apple crumble ice cream:

100g Sugar
100g Ground almonds
50g Flour
700g Cox apple
500g Vanilla ice cream base (see Basic Recipes)
100g Butter (frozen)

1. Pre-heat the oven to 160°C.

2. In a large bowl mix the sugar, almonds and flour. Grate the frozen butter into the bowl and using the tips of your fingers 'rub' the crumble mix together. Bake the crumble in a large oven dish until golden brown. You will have to cut through the mix a few times with a large spoon so the mix is cooked through.

3. As the crumble is cooking, peel and dice the apples. Add to a large saucepan with a splash of water and cook out until soft. Blend in a food processor and pass through a fine sieve. You need 50g of apple purée for the ice cream.

4. Mix the ice cream base, apple purée and the crumbs and blend in a food processor. Transfer to an ice cream machine and churn.

Other ingredients:

Citrus custard (see Basic Recipes)
20 Fresh blackberries
8 x Tuile baskets (see Basic Recipes)

To serve:

1. Rebake the soufflés for 7 minutes at 180°C.

2. Heat the custard and cut the clean blackberries in half.

3. Scoop the ice cream into the tuile baskets and place on the plates. Ladle a puddle of custard onto each plate with five pieces of blackberry around the custard. As soon as the soufflé is cooked, remove from the oven and place in the middle of the custard.

December January February

Scottish salmon with heritage beetroot vinaigrette, horseradish, fresh herbs & crème frâiche

Warm Golden Cross goats' cheese marinated in orange & honey with golden raisin, toasted pine nut & pear salad

Tasting of Gressingham duck; marinated breast, pâté on toast, pressed leg jelly & port reduction

Rump of Colne Valley lamb with Jerusalem artichoke & potato hot pot and purple sprouting broccoli

Rump and Wellington of dry-aged Hereford beef with wild mushroom duxelles, celeriac & red wine

Pheasant & onion pudding with creamed cabbage, chestnuts & local bacon

Gardeners pie topped with mashed potato, butternut purée, sprouting broccoli, roasted garlic & chilli oil

Spotted dick & custard with vanilla baked apple & rhubarb, vanilla ice cream

Fresh profiteroles filled with banana ice cream, warm chocolate sauce & caramelised hazelnuts

Scottish salmon with heritage beetroot vinaigrette, horseradish, fresh herbs & crème frâiche

Although salmon is not in season through the winter, the organic farmed fish are of such a good quality nowadays that I don't have an issue serving salmon through the winter, especially as most people will eat some type of salmon through the Christmas period.

Serves: 8

For the horseradish crème frâiche:
1kg Crème frâiche
10g Fresh horseradish
Salt and pepper

1. Hang the crème frâiche in a muslin cloth for 24 hours over a bowl in the fridge.

2. The next day, discard the liquid in the bowl and transfer to a clean mixing bowl.

3. Grate in the horseradish and season with salt and pepper. Mix.

For the salmon:
1kg Salmon fillet
Salt
Cayenne pepper
1kg Nage (see Basic Recipes)

1. Remove the skin from the salmon and season all over with freshly milled salt and cayenne pepper. Leave the salmon to rest for 2 hours in the fridge so that the salt and pepper can penetrate the fish.

2. Transfer the salmon to a container or a pan that is only just big enough to fit into. Bring the nage to the boil. Off the heat, and using a thermometer, allow the nage to cool to 75°C and then pour it over the salmon. Leave the salmon in the stock for 20 minutes, then very gently pour the nage away.

3. Return the just cooked salmon to the fridge to chill. When cold, portion the salmon into eight equal-sized pieces.

Other ingredients:
¼ bunch Dill
¼ bunch Chives
¼ bunch Chervil
1 tbsp Mustard
3 tbsp Water
5 Heritage beetroot (see Basic Recipes)
8 sprigs Chervil
100g Salmon keta

1. Pick all of the herbs from their stalks and cut the leaves very finely.

2. Mix the mustard and the water. Reserve until needed.

3. Slice the beetroot into 2mm slices on a mandolin. Using a 40mm cutter, cut each slice to a circle and then cut each circle in half.

4. Brush the top of each piece of salmon with the mustard/water mix and then push the salmon into the herbs so that one surface of the fish is completely covered.

To serve:

1. Place a quenelle of crème frâiche at the top of a cold plate.

2. Arrange the beetroot pieces in a circle at the bottom and place the salmon on top of the beetroot. Using two teaspoons quenelle the salmon keta onto the salmon. Finish the plate with a sprig of chervil.

Warm Golden Cross goats' cheese marinated in orange & honey with golden raisin, toasted pine nut & pear salad

Golden Cross is a lovely goats' cheese that has been rolled in ash so it develops a complexity as it matures. I like to use it for this dish as it can be warmed up particularly well.

Serves: 8

2 Golden Cross goats' cheese
3 tbsp Honey
50g Orange juice
100g Extra virgin olive oil
Zest of 1 orange
4 Pears

For the salad:
1 head Frisee
20g Basil cress
20g Chervil
20g Celery cress
20g Red vein sorrel
20g Pine nuts
20g Golden raisins
20g Croutons

1. Cut each cheese log into four equal pieces.

2. Mix the honey, orange juice, olive oil and the zest of the orange and pour it over the cheese. Marinate for 12 hours.

3. To make the salad, pick the nice young yellow leaves from the frisee and wash well. Using a salad spinner, dry the leaves.

4. In a large mixing bowl add the frisee, basil, chervil, celery cress, sorrel, pine nuts, raisins and the croutons. Carefully mix together.

5. Using a melon baller, remove the core from the bottom of the pears.

6. Cut each pear in half and slice to 2mm on a mandolin. Cut each slice in half.

7. Pre-heat the oven to 110°C.

8. Remove the cheese pieces from the marinade, place them on a tray and warm through in the oven for about 10 minutes. The cheese should just be starting to go soft, but be warm through.

9. Whilst the cheese is in the oven, just warm the marinade in a pan – Just warm, NOT hot!

10. Toss the salad.

To serve:

1. Arrange the pear slices all the way around each plate, leaving a hole in the middle big enough to put the cheese.

2. Remove the cheese from the oven and put on the middle of each plate. Scatter the salad around the edge of each plate and finish with some of the warm dressing.

Tasting of Gressingham duck; marinated breast, pâté on toast, pressed leg jelly & port reduction

Roasted duck epitomises winter as far as I'm concerned. I think it is the wonderful aroma of roasting duck fat that conjures up such a clear image in so many people's minds. Because duck is quite a sweet meat, it pairs so well with the festive spices and flavours that we all associate with Christmas. This starter uses every bit of the duck!

Serves: 6

2 Gressingham ducks –
remove the breasts, legs and
liver

For the leg rillettes:
2 Duck legs
Sea salt
2kg duck fat

For the duck breast:
2 Duck breasts
Orange
1 tbsp Honey
2 Star anise
2 tbsp Red wine
2 tbsp Red wine vinegar
2 sprigs Thyme
2 tbsp Extra virgin olive oil

1. Pre-heat the oven to 120°C.

2. Using a blow torch, burn any bits of feather that are left on the legs and then rub all over in salt. Rest the duck legs in the fridge for 4 hours to let the salt work its way into the duck.

3. Brush the excess salt from the duck legs, place in a deep roasting dish and cover with the duck fat. Bring the whole lot to the simmer, cover with greaseproof paper and tin foil and transfer to the oven to cook. The legs will take about 3 hours and are ready when the bones are falling away from the meat. When ready, take out of the oven, remove the foil and paper and allow the legs to cool in the duck fat, approximately 1 hour.

4. When cool enough to handle, carefully remove the bones from the meat and transfer the meat to a clean mixing bowl. Add to the bowl about half as much duck fat as there is meat and using two forks, shred the meat in the fat. It will form into a coarse pâté. Don't be put off by the amount of fat in there – it will taste utterly delicious!

5. Season to taste. Cover the rillettes with paper and keep cool until ready to serve.

6. Marinate the duck breast for 24 hours in orange, honey, star anise, red wine, vinegar, thyme and extra virgin olive oil.

Tasting of Gressingham duck; marinated breast, pâté on toast, pressed leg jelly & port reduction (continued)

For the duck liver parfait:
This will make more than you need, but it is about the smallest recipe that will work. One duck won't produce this much liver either, so you will have to purchase a little extra to make up the recipe.

For the reduction:
1 Small onion
60g Madeira
60g Port
30g Brandy

For the parfait:
225g Duck liver
200g Soft butter
2 Eggs
8g Salt

1. Pre-heat the oven to 110ºC.

2. Peel and slice the onion and mix it with the Madeira, port and brandy. On a gentle heat, reduce the alcohol until it has virtually all gone.

3. Add the livers to the reduction and blend until very smooth in a food processor. If you have a processor that you can control the temperature on, set it to 55ºC.

4. Add the butter bit by bit and continue to blend. Finally add the eggs and the salt. Blend until smooth then pass through a fine sieve.

5. Line a 500ml ovenproof mould with clingfilm and fill it with the parfait mix.

6. Bake the parfait in a 'bain marie' in the oven for approximately 20 minutes. To check it is done, insert a temperature probe – the parfait should be 63ºC in the centre.

7. Remove from the 'bain marie' and allow to cool in the fridge. When completely cool, transfer the parfait to a piping bag.

For the brioche soldiers:
2 slices of brioche

1. Slice the brioche into 1cm slices and toast. Cut into finger-width soldiers – you need 12 soldiers in total.

Other ingredients:
Zest of 1 orange
Cumberland dressing
(See wood pigeon recipe on page 119)
15 Leaves baby endive
24 x 4mm Discs of white radish
Chives
24 Sprigs chervil

1. Cook the duck breast under a grill, allowing the fat to slowly render out – be careful though, as the marinade will cause them to burn quite easily. Cook to 60ºC in the centre on a meat probe. Allow to rest for 5 minutes before slicing.

2. Pipe the duck parfait along each of the brioche toasts. Using a micro plane, grate orange zest over the parfait.

3. Slice the duck breasts into 12 slices each. In a large mixing bowl toss the sliced duck breast with a little Cumberland dressing, endive leaves, white radish discs and a few chives.

4. To serve, quenelle two spoons of the rillettes onto each plate. Arrange the duck breast and the salad neatly around. Finish with the brioche fingers and a little more Cumberland dressing.

Rump of Colne Valley lamb with Jerusalem artichoke & potato hot pot and purple sprouting broccoli

Don't be put off by garlic purée. Blanching the garlic a few times in boiling water will get rid of all of the bitterness and the resulting purée is delicate and creamy – and perfect with lamb rump.

Serves: 8

For the Jerusalem artichoke and potato hot pot:
200g Red onion
175g Lamb mince
25g Olive oil
3g Salt
330g Artichokes
165g Potato
¼ Bunch mint
5 Sprigs rosemary

1. Pre-heat the oven to 160ºC.

2. Peel and slice the red onions very finely. In a wide pan roast the onion and lamb mince in the olive oil and salt until golden brown. Remove from the heat.

3. Slice the peeled artichokes and potatoes on a mandolin and mix them with the herbs and the lamb mice mix.

3. Line a 15 x 20cm gratin dish with greaseproof paper. Neatly lattice the bottom two layers of the gratin dish with the sliced potatoes and artichokes – this will be the presentation side, so it wants to be neat and tidy. Once you have the first two layers done, you can be a bit more rustic in the layering process and almost scatter the mix in until the gratin is full and uniformly filled.

4. Line the top of the gratin with greaseproof paper and then place another gratin dish of the same size on top. The top dish will gently push down on the filling as it cooks, helping it all stay together when you come to serve. Place the two dishes in the oven and cook for about 40 minutes or until an inserted knife will pass through the potatoes with zero resistance.

For the garlic purée:
200g Garlic, peeled
Whipping cream
Salt and pepper, to taste

1. Place the garlic in a pan of cold water and bring to the boil.

2. Once boiled, discard the water and refill the pan with cold water and repeat the process (five times in total).

3. After the fifth boil, transfer the garlic to a food processor. Blitz until smooth adding a touch of whipping cream and seasoning as required.

4. Pass through a fine sieve into a clean pan ready for use.

For the scorched onions:
4 small onions
Olive oil
Salt and pepper

1. Pre-heat the oven to 200ºC.

2. With the skin still intact and cutting from the top, cut the onions into eight wedges, but don't cut all the way through. Stop just above the root of the onion so that they stay intact. Brush with a little olive oil and a twist of salt. Bake in the oven until the onion is tender. The outside will start to char (giving a lovely bittersweet taste to the finished onions).

3. Remove the onions from the oven and fully separate the scorched segments. Discard the skin.

Rump of Colne Valley lamb with Jerusalem artichoke & potato hot pot and purple sprouting broccoli (continued)

For the artichoke crisps:
8 Jerusalem artichokes

1. Peel and slice the artichokes on a mandolin.

2. Deep-fry at 170°C until golden and crisp.

3. Season with table salt.

For the lamb:
8 Rumps of Colne Valley lamb (about 200g each) – cross-hatch the skin
Lamb sauce (see Basic Recipes)

1. Pre-heat the oven to 180°C.

2. Heat a heavy-based pan with a little vegetable oil. Season the lamb rumps and start to caramelise the skin side. Carefully baste the oil over the flesh. Flip the lamb and colour the flesh side, again basting as you go.

3. Remove the lamb from the pan, tip out the fat and return the lamb, skin side down. Cover with foil and cook in the oven for about 8-10 minutes. The lamb should reach 63°C on a meat probe. Remove the lamb from the oven and allow to rest for 5 minutes.

For the broccoli:
16 Long spears purple broccoli

4. Place a cutting board over the potato gratin and, in one swift movement, flip the whole thing over so that the potato drops onto the board. Remove the paper, and portion into eight pieces with a sharp serrated knife.

5. Cook the broccoli in boiling salted water.

6. Slice the lamb rumps

To serve:

1. Swipe the garlic purée across your plates. Place the potato hot pot at the top of the plate with the broccoli sat next to it.

2. Place the sliced lamb rumps in the middle of the plate. Finish with lamb sauce and a few artichoke crisps.

Rump and Wellington of dry-aged Hereford beef with wild mushroom duxelles, celeriac & red wine

Not a classic version of this dish as we use braised beef to fill this Wellington. Braised beef and pastry make great comfort food in the colder months.

Serves: 8

For the Wellington:
500g Beef, diced
Roasted garlic pulp (see Basic Recipes)
4 Sprigs thyme
500g Veal stock
250g Caramelised onions (see Basic Recipes)
300g Puff pastry (see Basic Recipes)
1 Egg

1. You can prepare the Wellington the day before, everything else can be cooked on the day.

2. Pre-heat the oven to 150ºC.

3. In a wide pan, with a little vegetable oil, roast the diced beef until deep brown. Tip out the oil and add the garlic and thyme.

4. Transfer the beef to a large casserole dish and add the veal stock. Bring the stock to the simmer, pop on the lid and cook in the oven until the meat is very tender, approximately 2 hours.

5. When cooked, allow the beef to cool for 30 minutes before removing it from the casserole. Pass the cooking liquid into a clean saucepan and reduce by three-quarters. Shred the beef and mix it with the caramelised onions and the reduced beef cooking liquid. Adjust the seasoning.

6. Lay a double sheet of clingfilm on a work surface and, working on the clingfilm, shape the beef mix into a sausage shape about 3cm in diameter. Roll up the sausage in the clingfilm and place into the fridge to set.

7. Roll the puff pastry to a neat rectangle 30cm x 10cm. Cover with clingfilm and rest in the fridge for 30 minutes. Once rested, beat the egg and brush over one side.

8. Take the beef from the fridge, place it in the middle of the puff pastry and roll over to seal. Trim off any excess pastry and brush the top with more egg wash. Lightly season with Maldon sea salt. Transfer the Wellington to a baking sheet, ready to cook.

For the beef steaks:
6 x 170g Portions Hereford beef rump
1 tbsp Roasted garlic pulp (see Basic Recipes)
6 Sprigs picked thyme
50g Olive oil

1. Season the beef all over with salt and pepper and allow to sit at room temperature for 25 minutes.

2. Mix the roast garlic, picked thyme and olive oil. Dry the beef with kitchen towel and then brush over the garlic-thyme mix. Allow to marinate on a plate until you are ready to cook.

For the celeriac purée:
700g Celeriac
200g Whipping cream
Maldon sea salt
Truffle oil

1. Remove the outer skin from the celeriac and slice as finely as possible. Season and add to the saucepan with the cream and cook out over a medium heat with a lid on until the celeriac is very tender.

2. Blend the mix in a food processor until very smooth and add a few drops of truffle oil. Adjust the seasoning as required and pass through a fine sieve.

Rump and Wellington of dry-aged Hereford beef with wild mushroom duxelles, celeriac & red wine (continued)

For the mushroom duxelles:
200g Small onion, sliced
1kg Mushrooms, sliced
Bay leaf and thyme (tied together)
80g Butter
50g Madeira
50g Double cream

1. In a wide pan, sweat the onions, mushrooms and the herbs in the butter until dry, with a little colour (golden).

2. Deglaze with the Madeira, add the splash of cream and reduce just a little.

3. Remove the bay and thyme, and pulse chop in a food processor. Adjust the seasoning.

For the dripping vegetables:
250g Celery
250g Carrot
250g Celeriac
50g Beef dripping
50g Curly parsley

1. Peel the vegetables and slice first on a mandolin to 5mm, then cut each slice to 5mm dice. Toss the vegetables in a little sea salt and then cook in a steaming pan for approximately 2 minutes or until just cooked.

2. Tip the vegetables onto a tray and allow to cool. Once cool, transfer to a pan.

Other ingredients:
500g Red wine sauce (see Basic Recipes)

To serve:

1. Pre-heat the oven to 180°C with a baking sheet inside.

2. Slide the Wellington on to the hot baking sheet and cook for 30 minutes. The hot tray will start cooking the pastry from underneath straight away and will prevent you ending up with a soggy bottom.

3. Reheat the celeriac purée.

4. Heat the diced vegetables and when hot, add the dripping and the chopped parsley. The parsley will absorb the fat and the mix should all start to stick together.

5. Reheat the duxelles in a pan.

6. Cook the beef on a chargrill, turning every 30 seconds or so, so that it cooks evenly. If using a temperature probe, the centre wants to reach 56°C for medium rare. Rest the beef in a warm place with foil over for 3 or 4 minutes. Slice the beef and season with freshly milled salt and pepper.

7. Remove the Wellington from the oven and portion into eight pieces.

9. On a warm plate, using a spoon swipe the celeriac purée along one side. Make a quenelle with the duxelles and place next to the top of the purée. Quenelle the vegetables and place next to the duxelles. Place the Wellington next to the vegetables. Finish with the sliced beef and red wine sauce.

Pheasant & onion pudding with creamed cabbage, chestnuts & local bacon

Pheasant legs can be a nuisance. I don't care what anyone says, they do not make a good eat as a whole leg. Delicious they may be, but there is too much bone and ligament to be enjoyable. Pheasants, they come with the legs though, and so need to be used. This is my way of using them up.

Serves: 4

2 Bottles red wine
10 Pheasant legs
¼ Bunch thyme
2 Bay leaves
50g Carrots
50g Onions
50g Mushrooms
100g Smoked bacon
4kg Veal stock
Red wine vinegar
100g Caramelised onions
(see Basic Recipes)

1. Pour the bottle of red wine into a container and add the legs with the thyme and bay leaf. Marinate in the fridge for 24 hours.

2. On the day of cooking, pre-heat the oven to 120°C.

3. Remove the pheasant legs from the marinade, pat dry on a tea towel and discard the wine. Season the meat all over with table salt and rest for 30 minutes.

4. In a wide shallow pan or roasting dish, add a good lug of vegetable oil and on a high heat, fry the legs on the skin side until caramelised all over – it should be a deep mahogany colour. Transfer the meat to a deep casserole dish and now (in the same pan) roughly chop and fry the carrots, onion, mushrooms and smoked bacon. When golden, tip all of the contents of the pan through a colander sat over a bowl. The fat collected in the bowl can be discarded and the vegetables and bacon added to the casserole dish.

5. Deglaze the original pan with the last bottle of red wine and reduce by half, then pour the contents into the casserole. Add the veal stock to just cover. On a medium heat bring the contents of the casserole to the simmer, and then put the lid on and transfer to the oven. Cook until the meat is very tender – approximately 2 hours. When cooked, remove the lid and let the casserole cool down for 1 hour. Gently lift the meat from the pot and transfer it to a tray. Pass the liquid through a colander into a clean pan – discard the vegetables and bacon – they will have imparted all of their flavour.

6. Over a medium heat reduce the pheasant liquid until it is thick and sticky. Whilst the stock is reducing, shred the pheasant meat and pick out any gristle and bones. Take your time as this is not as easy as it sounds and there are lots of fiddly little bits to remove.

7. Once the stock has reduced, mix it with the shredded meat, caramelised onions, a few drops of red wine vinegar and any seasoning if it is required.

Pheasant & onion pudding with creamed cabbage, chestnuts & local bacon (continued)

To make the suet pastry puddings:
200g Plain flour
50g Suet
Pinch of dried thyme
60g Butter, diced
40g Water (approximately)
6g Maldon sea salt

1. In a food processor, cut the flour, suet, thyme and butter to 'breadcrumbs'. Add the water and pulse mix to just incorporate.

2. Turn out on to a board, knead to form a uniform dough. Chill.

3. Cut the dough into four equal pieces. Now cut each piece into two but have one piece two-thirds the size of the other.

4. Line four third-pint (190ml) pudding bowls with soft butter and flour. Gently tap out any excess flour.

5. Roll the suet pastry into discs – there should be four big ones and four smaller ones. Line the inside of each bowl with the larger suet pastry disc. Gently knead out any creases with your fingers. Carefully fold the excess pastry down the side of the bowl, but don't cut it off.

6. Now fill each mould with the pheasant leg mix. Brush the smaller disc of pastry with a little water and crimp it on top of the pies. Trim off any excess pastry and, using a pair of scissors, snip a cross in the middle of each lid. Now brush with egg wash, and season with Maldon sea salt.

For the creamed cabbage:
1 Carrot
50g Celeriac
1 Small onion
½ Leek
50g Smoked back bacon
1 Savoy cabbage
50g Butter
50g Double cream
Salt and pepper

1. Cut the carrot, celeriac, onion, leek, and bacon into a small neat dice.

2. Take the core from the cabbage and shred.

3. To cook the cabbage, melt the butter in a pan and add the vegetable and bacon dice, sweat out on a high heat, stirring all the time so that they don't catch and burn.

4. Add the cabbage, cream and seasoning to the pan and cook until the cabbage is cooked and the cream is just coating. Be generous with the black pepper when serving.

For the chestnut purée:
120g Chestnuts
12g Butter
Salt
Sugar
125g Chicken stock
75g Milk

1. Fry the chestnuts in butter with a sprinkle of salt and sugar, add the chicken stock and milk bring to the simmer. Cover with a lid and cook out for 30 minutes.

2. Blend in a food processor. Pass through a fine sieve into a clean pan.

To serve:

1. Pre-heat the oven to 180°C.

2. Cook the pheasant puddings for 25 minutes.

3. Swipe the chestnut purée across a plate.

4. Mould the cabbage to a neat circle using a metal ring and place the pheasant pudding on top. Serve the sauce (you will need 250g of pheasant sauce – see Basic Recipes) on the side in a little pan so that it does not mix with the cream from the cabbage until the last moment.

Gardeners pie topped with mashed potato, butternut purée, sprouting broccoli, roasted garlic & chilli oil

A take on Shepherd's pie, but using winter root vegetables in place of lamb. This is a nice hearty dish packed with flavour and a little spice.

Serves: 4

For the pudding:
300g Vegan pastry (see Basic Recipes)
Olive oil, for frying
¼ Butternut squash
½ Swede
3 Carrots
1 Small onion
1 tsp Cumin seeds
Salt and pepper, to season
1 tsp Roasted garlic pulp (see Basic Recipes)

1. Cut the pastry dough into four equal pieces. Line four third-pint (190ml) pudding bowls with soft butter and flour. Gently tap out any excess flour.

2. Roll the pastry into four discs – this pastry is very soft, so work in a cool environment and use the pastry straight from the fridge. Line the inside of each bowl with the pastry and gently knead out any creases with your fingers. Chill until needed.

3. Peel and prepare the vegetables to 1cm dice.

4. In a wide pan heat some olive oil and fry off the vegetable dice until a golden roast colour is achieved. Add the cumin, seasoning and garlic to the pan, turn the heat down and put on a lid. Continue to cook until the vegetables are just cooked, not mush!

5. Chill the vegetables before filling up the moulds.

For the butternut squash purée:
1 Butternut squash
Salt and pepper, to season
100g Whipping cream
Fresh nutmeg

1. Remove the outer skin from the squash, chop in half and remove the seeds. Slice as finely as possible. Add the butternut and seasoning to a saucepan with the cream and cook out over a medium heat with a lid on until very tender.

2. Blend the mix in a food processor until very smooth. Adjust the seasoning as required, rasp in some fresh nutmeg and pass through a fine sieve.

For the honey roast parsnips and broccoli:
6 Parsnips
12 Spears purple broccoli
½ tsp Harissa
1 tsp Honey
1 tsp Sesame seeds
Olive oil

1. Peel the parsnips and cut into quarters lengthways. Using a small paring knife cut out the woody stalk from each piece of parsnip.

2. Mix the harissa, honey and sesame seeds with some olive oil.

Other ingredients:

*Mashed potatoes, to crisp
(see Basic Recipes)
Spinach*

1. Pre-heat the oven to 180ºC.

2. Trim the excess pastry from the pies and using a bag fitted with a star nozzle, pipe the mashed potato 'Walnut Whip' style on top. Bake in the oven for 30 minutes.

3. While the pie is cooking slowly roast the parsnips in olive oil. Take your time, so that they colour evenly. When golden in colour, add the honey, sesame and harissa. Continue cooking until the parsnips are golden and sticky.

4. In a separate steamer pan cook the broccoli for just 1 minute and then add to the parsnips. Remove from the heat and roll all around together.

5. Wilt enough spinach for four portions.

6. Put the butternut squash purée on each plate and using the back of a ladle, swirl it out to a neat circle. Place the drained spinach on the purée and put the cooked pie on top.

7. Arrange the spicy broccoli and parsnip next to the pies.

Spotted dick & custard with vanilla baked apple & rhubarb, vanilla ice cream

I adore steamed sponges and don't think that there is any greater comfort food. Spotted dick for me is the king of sponges, it's not too sweet, there is texture from the fruit, and you feel totally satisfied after eating. I like to serve a sponge with custard and ice cream.

Serves: 6

For the spotted dick sponge:
160g Plain flour
10g Baking powder
80g Chopped suet
38g Caster sugar
55g Currants
Zest of 1 lemon
1 Vanilla pod
95g Milk

1. In a large bowl, mix the flour, baking powder, suet, caster sugar, currants, lemon zest and scraped vanilla seeds. Add the milk and knead to form a soft dough.

2. Line individual pudding moulds (250ml) with butter, and dust with plain flour. Spoon the mixture into the moulds (70g per mould) and place a piece of folded greaseproof paper over the top. Secure with an elastic band.

3. Put the puddings in a steamer pan with plenty of water in it. On full heat, steam the puddings for 50 minutes. For best results have the steamer on full heat but be sure to check the water level periodically – and don't let the pan boil dry!

For the fruit:
3 Sticks rhubarb
2 Cox apples
20g Butter
½ Vanilla pod

1. Pre-heat the oven to 160°C.

2. Trim the ends off the rhubarb, wash well and cut into an even 1cm dice. Peel the apples and cut to the same size as the rhubarb.

3. In a roasting dish, melt the butter and scrape in the vanilla seeds from the pod. Add the fruit and cover with foil. Bake in the oven until the rhubarb and the apple is just starting to soften, about 5 minutes, but check with the spike of a knife as the rhubarb, especially, will overcook very quickly. When ready, remove from the oven and keep warm.

Other ingredients:
Custard (see Basic Recipes)
Vanilla ice cream (see Basic Recipes)
6 x Tuile baskets (see Basic Recipes)

1. In a warm bowl, place alternate pieces of apple and rhubarb in a circle.

2. Pour in a ladle of custard and place the steamed pudding on top.

3. Finish with a tuile basket with vanilla ice cream inside.

Fresh profiteroles filled with banana ice cream, warm chocolate sauce & caramelised hazelnuts

I am not a big fan of chocolate. It doesn't very often offer much of a surprise, you know what you are going to get. That being the case, any chocolate dessert needs to just be an absolute crowd pleaser, a treat of gluttony. This is one such dessert.

Serves: 8

For the chocolate sauce:
100g Water
140g Whipping cream
57g Cocoa powder
114g Sugar
43g Chocolate buttons (70%)
36g Butter

1. In a small pan on a gentle heat, bring the water, cream, cocoa and sugar to the boil.

2. Remove from the heat and whisk in the chocolate and the butter. Pass through a fine sieve into a clean pan for later use.

For the banana ice cream:
450g Milk
5 Bananas, peeled and sliced
250g Double cream
125g Glucose
40g Trimoline
4 Egg yolks
100g Sugar
50g Banana liquor

1. Bring the milk to the boil.

2. Add the sliced banana and remove from the heat. Cover with clingfilm and rest for 10 minutes. Pass through a colander and discard the banana.

3. In a kitchen mixer, whisk the egg yolks, sugar and liquor to make a sabayon. It needs to double in volume.

4. Mix the banana milk with the cream, glucose and trimoline and bring to the boil. Add one large ladle of the boiling liquid to the sabayon, and whisk the two together. Now tip the sabayon into the boiling liquid, whisking as you go. Continue to whisk until the custard has thickened and reaches 75°C on a thermometer.

5. Remove from the heat and continue to whisk for at least 2 minutes. Cool the pan down in a sink filled with cold water, and whisk for 2 more minutes. Pass the ice cream base though a fine sieve and chill in the fridge. Churn in an ice cream maker.

For the praline:

200g Caster sugar
200g Peeled hazelnuts

1. Pre-heat the oven to 160°C.

2. In a heavy pan, melt the sugar and then cook out to a caramel (177°C on a thermometer).

3. Whilst the sugar is coming up to caramel, lightly roast the hazelnuts until golden brown in the oven.

4. Add the hot hazelnuts to the caramel and mix in. If the nuts are cold it will cause the caramel to 'freeze' and set before you can mix them in properly.

5. Tip the praline onto greaseproof paper and allow to set properly – this takes a surprisingly long time, approximately 30 minutes at least. When set, use a rolling pin to smash the praline into little pieces.

For the profiteroles:

250g Water
80g Butter
10g Sugar
2g Salt
150g Flour
4 Eggs

1. Pre-heat the oven to 200°C.

2. Bring the water, butter, sugar and salt to the boil. Remove from the heat and beat in the flour. When smooth, return the pan to the heat and over a high heat, cook out for 1 minute. Transfer the mix to the bowl of a food mixer, and on a low speed using the 'K' beater, mix the dough until it has cooled, approximately 5 minutes.

3. Now start adding the eggs one at a time, not adding the next egg until the first has been fully incorporated.

4. Lightly grease a large baking sheet. Using a piping bag and plain 1cm nozzle, pipe the mixture into small balls in lines across the baking sheet. Transfer the baking sheet into the oven. Bake for 25-30 minutes or until golden brown.

To serve:

1. Allowing three profiteroles per person, cut them all in half. Using an ice cream scoop, place a small ball of banana ice cream on the bottom half of each profiterole. Place the top half on top of the ice cream and place three profiteroles in the centre of each plate.

2. Drizzle over the warm chocolate sauce and finish with the hazelnut praline crumbs.

*Fresh profiteroles filled with
banana ice cream, warm chocolate
sauce & caramelised hazelnuts*

Basic Recipes

Bread

Fresh bread is very much taken for granted in society today, and with the everlasting loaves and negative press about gluten, bread does not get the credit it deserves. Wheat has kept man alive for thousands of years, and for it to suddenly be a problem in our diet does not wash with me. I like very simple bread, fresh and warm, with some lovely salted butter to start a meal. If you are buying flour from a supermarket I would strongly recommend Shipton Mill – it does not have any unnecessary additives.

Bread is very simple to make and very rewarding. Rolling the bread is one of my favourite jobs at Albert's Table.

The below method for all of the following breads is the same:

1. Mix all of the ingredients in a large bowl, or using a dough machine. As soon as smooth dough is formed, stop mixing and cover the dough with clingfilm and leave to double in size.

2. Pre-heat the oven to 220ºC. If you have an option to add steam then do, if not, put a pan of hot water at the bottom of the oven.

3. When the dough is well risen (about 20 minutes, depending on the temperature of the kitchen), knock back the dough and either turn into a loaf tin, or pull off 35g lumps and form into rolls.

4. Place the rolls onto a greased baking tray, dust with flour and score with a knife. Cover with clingfilm and allow to prove again until they look plum.

5. When ready, remove the clingfilm and slide into the oven. Cook for 3 minutes and then turn the baking sheet around and bake for another 3 minutes.

6. Let the bread rest for 5 minutes to cool down before eating.

7. Fresh bread will go stale within 24 hours.

Raisin & fennel seed

Makes 20 rolls (35g each)

38g Fresh yeast
600g T55 flour
18g Olive oil
27g Honey
145g Raisins
20g Maldon sea salt
9g Fennel seeds
335g Water

Spelt bread

Makes 20 rolls (35g each)

38g Fresh yeast
440g Spelt flour
220g White flour
17g Maldon sea salt
90g Greek yoghurt
7g Honey
335g Water

White potato & rosemary

Makes 20 rolls (35g each)

55g Fresh yeast
633g T55 flour
60g Olive oil
17g Salt
33g Honey
67g Steamed mashed potato
8g Dried rosemary
310g Water

Gluten-free bread

Due to popular demand, we do produce a gluten-free bread at the restaurant. I have tried literally hundreds of recipes and have always been disappointed. A lot of GF recipes taste more like a cake than bread, or they call for gum products to help give elasticity to doughs. I am not at all keen on cooking with gums.

After some lengthy research, I discovered the elasticity properties of linseeds and psyllium husk. This bread is very good, although you may have to hunt the health food shops to get all of the ingredients.

Makes 20 rolls (35g each)

50g Golden linseeds
475g Warm water
74g Yeast
100g Natural yoghurt
450g Cornflower
22g Salt
45g Honey
50g Psyllium husk powder
50g Olive oil
Extra olive oil and cornflour, to finish

1. Pre-heat the oven to 170°C.

2. Bake a tray of the linseeds for 10-12 minutes or until they darken slightly (toasting will burst the husks slightly and allow the seeds to release a sticky gluten-like gum when wet, making the crumb softer and adding a wheat germ-like flavour).

3. Blend the linseeds in a food processor.

4. Measure out the correct amount of linseeds in a large bowl and combine the rest of the ingredients. Mix with a dough hook for 5 minutes until a soft dough is formed.

5. Cover with clingfilm and rest for 30 minutes.

6. Grease a tray as normal and shape the bread. Slash the top with a sharp knife and sprinkle with a little cornflour to give it a floured look. Cover and leave to rise for 30 minutes.

7. Uncover the dough and bake for 4 + 4 minutes at 220°C steam heat.

Focaccia

Focaccia is a wonderfully light bread dough flavoured with olive oil and sea salt. I like to cook it as a large flat loaf. For an extra treat, mix roasted vegetables through the dough – it tastes fabulous.

750g T45 flour
350g Water
100g Olive oil
17g Yeast
25g Maldon sea salt
8g Sugar
½ Bunch sage, chopped

1. Pre-heat oven to 200°C.

2. Mix all of the ingredients with a dough hook on a food processor.

3. Rub a baking dish (approximately 20cm x 30cm) with olive oil. Turn the dough into the dish, and using the palm of your hand, push the dough to completely cover the dish.

4. Brush the top with olive oil.

5. Using your fingers, push holes all over the surface then sprinkle the top with sea salt. Lightly cover with clingfilm and leave in a warm place to prove and double in size.

6. Remove the clingfilm. Place in the oven and cook for 20 minutes.

Shortcrust pastry

Shortcrust is super versatile, gloriously delicious and not as time consuming to make as other savoury pastries. It is not difficult to make, but like most things, to make it really well does require a bit of care. The end product should be crumbly, soft and rich.

The secret to good pastry is not overworking the flour once the liquid is added.

In its dry state the flour does not 'work' very much, so it is best to get all of the fats fully combined before adding any liquid. A little lard with the butter gives a truly decadent texture to pastry, but you can substitute margarine if you are not keen on lard.

Pastry will keep for a few days in the fridge, or freeze to have ready in the future.

Enough to line 9-inch tart case

375g Flour
38g Lard/margarine
200g Butter
4g Salt
50g Water

1. Freeze the butter and the lard.

2. In a mixing bowl sift in the flour and the salt. Coarsely grate in the butter and lard. Grating in the fats creates a very large surface area to volume to allow the flour to stick to, allowing the two ingredients to combine more easily and uniformly.

3. Select the medium speed on a food mixer, and using the 'K' beater, mix the flour and fat until it resembles breadcrumbs.

4. Add the water and continue to mix until the crumbs start to come together.

5. Stop the mixer immediately. Overmixing at this point will overwork the flour.

6. Turn the dough out onto a work surface and just bring it all together into a ball.

7. Cut the ball in half, and wrap in clingfilm. At this point the pastry is good to go.

8. Alternatively, wrap the pastry in clingfilm and rest in the fridge. I always think that overnight is a safe move and the pastry will keep in the fridge for a week anyway. Always keep it wrapped so that it does not take on the smells of the fridge.

Vegan shortcrust

Enough to line 9-inch tart case

375g Flour
238g Margarine*
4g Salt
50g Water

1. Other than not needing to freeze the margarine, the method for vegan pastry is the same as for normal shortcrust pastry (see above).

*The dough will be quite soft depending on the brand of margarine used, and also be careful that your margarine is completely dairy free.

Blind Baking

1. Pre-heat the oven to 170°C.

2. Roll out the shortcrust (or vegan) pastry and line a 9-inch tart case.

3. Line with greaseproof paper and fill with baking beans, making sure that the beans are pushed right into the corners of the tart.

4. Rest for 30 minutes in the fridge.

5. Resting pastry is very important. Although you can't see any physical changes, the way it cooks will be completely different; unrested pastry will 'shrink' as it cooks.

6. 'Blind bake' for 35 minutes, or until the base of the pastry has started to firm up and won't lift when the beans are removed. For best results when blind baking, don't use a fan oven.

7. When a firm base has been achieved, remove the beans and the paper and cook for a further 7 minutes to get a really crisp base.

8. The pastry case is now ready for a whole manner of delightful fillings and will stay crisp to the end.

Flaky pastry

220g Butter
350g Plain flour
Pinch of table salt
60g Water

1. Wrap the butter in foil and freeze.

2. Sift the flour and salt into a large bowl.

3. Taking the block of butter out of the freezer, peel back the foil and grate on the coarse setting into the flour, dipping the edge of the butter into the flour several times to ease the grating. With a palette knife, distribute the gratings of butter in to the flour.

4. Sprinkle in the water all over the flour mix. Continue with the palette knife until the mix comes together. Finish with hands to bring to a ball.

5. Wrap and chill.

Puff pastry

Fresh puff pastry is incomparable to shop bought. In my mind, freshly cooked puff pastry is one of the most delicious things to eat. It is not difficult to make, but it is time consuming. This recipe will make 3 x 400g blocks. If you are going to make it, make a full recipe, and freeze down what you do not use.

For the dough:
500g Flour
250g Water
12g Salt
1 tsp White wine vinegar
50g Butter, melted

For the pomade:
120g Flour
400g butter, diced

1. For the dough, mix the ingredients together.

2. Roll into a ball and slice a cross in the top. Wrap in clingfilm and chill in the fridge.

3. To make the pomade, beat the flour and butter until combined. Roll to A5 paper size. Wrap in clingfilm and chill in the fridge.

4. Take the dough and roll to slightly larger than A4 size.

5. Place the chilled pomade at one end and then wrap around the dough so it looks like a book.

6. Place in front of you – it should look like a closed book – and roll so that it is three times as long as it is wide. Fold it into thirds – the dough should be square. Wrap and chill.

7. Repeat this process four more times; always start with the dough placed like a closed book, with the opening on your right, five turns in total.

Basic pasta dough

Working fresh pasta is a true labour of love. Make sure you have the time and patience!

Salt
300g 'OO' flour
2 Eggs
3 Egg yolks
10g Olive oil

1. Blend the salt and flour in a food processor. Add the eggs, yolks and olive oil. The dough should go to breadcrumb texture. Turn the machine off and turn the dough onto a work surface. Knead the crumbs to form a smooth dough. Wrap in clingfilm and store in the fridge.

2. Using a rolling pin on a floured work surface, roll the pasta dough thin enough that it will fit into the thickest setting of a pasta machine.

3. Roll the dough through on number 10. Turn the setting down to 6 and pass the pasta through again. Fold the sheet of pasta into 3 and fire through the pasta machine on number 10. Turn the setting down to 6 and pass the pasta through again. This folding and rolling process needs to be performed about eight times. Now, starting on number 10, roll the dough through once at each setting until you end up at the desired thickness. The pasta is now ready to use.

Gougeres

I like to serve these little savoury puffs of cheesiness to all of our guests in the evening whilst they wait for their starters to be prepared. At home if I am having guests to dinner, I pop a whole pile of them in a basket in the middle of the table for everyone to dig in as they please.

250g Milk
250g Water
200g Butter
16g Salt
300g Flour
7 Eggs
200g Gruyere cheese

1. Pre-heat the oven to 230°C.

2. Heat the milk, water, butter and salt in a pan until combined. Take off the heat and mix in the flour. Return to the heat and cook out (about 3 minutes). Remove from the heat and allow to cool.

3. Using a food mixer with the paddle attachment, add the eggs one at a time. Fold in the cheese.

4. Transfer the mixture to a piping bag and pipe the gougeres onto a greased baking sheet lined with greaseproof paper and slide into the oven. Turn it down to 170°C.

5. Cook for 15-20 minutes until they are golden brown.

6. Allow to cool on tray.

7. Reheat in an oven for 1-2 minutes when ready to serve.

Gluten-free gougeres

Like the gluten-free bread, we used to struggle for something gluten-free to serve with the gougeres. This recipe is so good that we ONLY serve gluten-free gougeres now.

280g Milk
280g Water
220g Butter
18g Salt
18g Linseeds
164g Cornflour
18g Psyllium husk
8 Eggs
220g Gruyere cheese
1 tbsp English mustard

1. Pre-heat the oven to 230°C.

2. Heat the milk, water, butter and salt in pan, just enough to melt the butter. Do not let it boil.

3. Mix the 'flours' (linseeds, cornflour, psyllium husk) together, then off the heat, add to the milk mix and combine. Return to the heat and cook out only until it thickens, then stop straight away. Remove from the heat and tip onto a tray to cool.

4. Using a food mixer with paddle attachment, add the eggs one at a time. Fold in the cheese.

5. Transfer the mixture to a piping bag and pipe the gougeres on to a greased baking sheet lined with greaseproof paper and slide into the oven. Turn it down to 170°C.

6. Cook for 15 minutes until they are golden brown.

7. Allow to cool on the tray.

8. Reheat in an oven for 1-2 minutes when ready to serve.

Pesto

70g Basil
70g Roasted pine nuts
1 Garlic clove
140g Olive oil
70g Old Winchester cheese
or Parmesan, grated
Salt and pepper, to season

1. Blend the basil leaves, pine nuts, garlic and olive oil to a fine paste.

2. Fold in the grated cheese and adjust the seasoning as required.

House dressing

1 tsp Dijon mustard
50g Red wine vinegar
3g Salt
7g Sugar
50g Olive oil
150g Vegetable oil

1. In a large bowl, thoroughly whisk the mustard, vinegar, salt and sugar.

2. Slowly add the oils, whisking as you go to fully emulsify the dressing.

Crackling

This may seem a bit long winded for crackling, but it makes the best crackling ever.

1. Cover the pork skin with duck fat and confit for 6 hours at 120°C, or until completely soft.

2. Allow to cool in the fat and then lift on to a roasting rack. Season the pork skin with table salt and rest for 10 minutes – don't be tempted to use sea salt; it does not have the same effect in crisping the skin.

3. Pre-heat the oven to 180°C.

4. Either cut the skin into strips or leave whole.

5. Roast in the oven on a roasting rack until golden and crisp all over, approximately 40 minutes.

6. There will be lots of dripping that comes out during the roasting, so be sure to have a deep enough roasting tray under the rack to catch all of the fat.

Shellfish bisque

1kg Crayfish/Langoustine/
Gurnard/crab bones or shells
150g Butter
2 Carrots
1 Onion
2 Celery sticks
½ Fennel bulb
½ Leek
100g Brandy
2 tsp Harissa
0.5g Saffron
2 Garlic cloves
1 Bay leaf
4 Sprigs thyme
½ Bunch basil stalks

1. In a heavy-based wide pan, roast the bones in butter to a good colour.

2. Add the carrot and onion and continue to roast until the vegetables have colour – you may need to turn the heat down. Add the rest of the veg.

3. Deglaze the pan with the brandy. Add the harissa and the saffron and cook out for 5 minutes.

4. Pour everything into a small pan. Just cover with water and bring to the boil.

5. Add the garlic, bay and thyme and cook out for 20 minutes.

6. Rest for a further 20 minutes off the heat and pass through a fine sieve. Add the basil stalks and pass though a muslin.

7. Reduce to desired flavour and consistency. Adjust the seasoning.

Nage (vegetable stock)

I use a lot of vegetable stock at the restaurant. On its own it is not particularity exciting, but made with care, it is a very versatile ingredient, especially for vegetable work that we want to keep free from animal products.

3kg Mirepoix (onion, carrot,
fennel, celery, mushroom,
leek) sliced on Magimix
1 Head garlic
4kg Water
50g White wine
Pinch of chilli flakes
Herb stalks
Zest of 2 lemons
2 tbsp Coriander seeds
2 tbsp Fennel seeds
1 Star anise

1. Sweat all the mirepoix ingredients in a little butter or olive oil. Very lightly season.

2. Place the lid on the saucepan and cook out until the vegetables have started to wilt and soften.

3. Add the water and bring to the boil.

4. As soon as it reaches the boil, add the remaining ingredients and remove from the heat. Replace the lid and rest off of the heat for 20 minutes.

5. Pass through a colander. Let it sit for 10 minutes to drip through – do not force the stock though.

6. Pass through sieve. Chill.

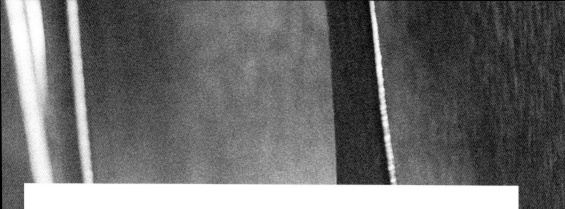

Sauces

Making a sauce is the last section a chef will work on in a professional kitchen. The guy on the sauce is the main man or woman, and he needs to get it right.

Knocking up a sauce is easy, to make it sparkle and shine takes a lot of practice and skill – rubbish stock, rubbish sauce. Cook it too long and it tastes dull, undercook it and it tastes of nothing. Over reduce and it is thick and sticky, under reduce it and it is like water… The list goes on.

In all honesty I would never try to cook a jus based sauce at home, a domestic kitchen is just not up to the job. Even preparing a good stock is nearly impossible at home – I don't know many people that have a pan big enough to cook out 10kg of bones!

Although I don't expect many people to be able to replicate these recipes, they can easily be adapted to give a very tasty compromise. Follow the first half of the recipe that is essentially adding the flavour to the sauce, and then add a simple stock and thicken it with cornflour to make a really flavoursome gravy. Of course add any meat juices that you have too.

I have included here the basic meat-based sauces that we make at Albert's Table. This is exactly how we make them, the basic principle for them all is the same.

We only use 'blond' stocks in the kitchen – bones and water, nothing else – and cook them out; chicken 12 hours, beef 20 hours. We then pass the stocks through a sieve and reduce them by half. The reason we do not add anything to our stocks is that it is just the gelatinous content that I am after.

Because of the way we buy our meat, we always have trim, and it is important to me that the sauces taste of the animal that they came from, and not just the alcohol that they are made with.

We add the flavour to our sauces by frying off all of the trim that we have for each sauce with carrots, onions and mushrooms, before we add the stock. The result is a very fresh sauce that adds real flavour to the meat that it is being served with.

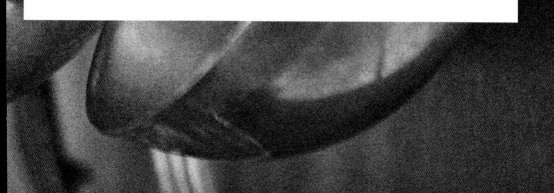

Beef

4kg Trim
200g Shallots
200g Mushrooms
200g Carrots
150g Cabernet sauvignon
red wine vinegar
1 Bottle red wine
1 Bottle port
6kg Veal stock
2 Sprigs thyme
1 Garlic bulb
1 Bay leaf
Salt and pepper, to taste

1. Cut the vegetables to a mirepoix.

2. Fry the trim in plenty of oil, until well coloured.

3. Add the vegetables and colour. When all is golden brown, pass into a big colander and allow oil to disperse.

4. Return the pan to the heat and deglaze with the red wine vinegar. Reduce by half.

5. Add the red wine and reduce by half.

6. Add the port and reduce by half.

7. Return the meat and vegetables to the pan. Add the stock and herbs and bring to the simmer. Cook out for 2 hours – do not let it boil.

8. Remove from the heat and rest for 20 minutes.

9. With a ladle, gently pass through a colander to a clean pan. Allow all the sauce to drip through.

10. Reduce to consistency and again with a ladle, gently pass through a sieve – do not force.

11. Finish with a splash of the red wine vinegar if needed and adjust seasoning.

12. Pass and chill.

Pork

4kg Trim
200g Shallots
200g Mushrooms
200g Carrots
150g Sherry vinegar
200g White wine
200g Madeira
6kg Pork (or chicken) stock
2 Sprigs thyme
1 Garlic bulb
1 Bay leaf
Salt and pepper, to taste

1. Cut the vegetables to a mirepoix.

2. Fry the trim in plenty of oil until well coloured. Though be careful; I take white meat to the colour of 'cornflakes', no further (any scorch will give a bitter taste to the sauce).

3. Add the vegetables, and colour. When all is golden brown, pass into a big colander and allow the oil to disperse.

4. Return the pan to the heat and deglaze with the sherry vinegar. Reduce by half.

5. Add the white wine and reduce by half.

6. Add the Madeira and reduce by half.

7. Return the meat and vegetables to the pan. Add the stock and the herbs and bring to the simmer. Cook out for 2 hours – do not let it boil.

8. Remove from the heat and rest for 20 minutes.

9. With a ladle, gently pass through colander to a clean pan. Allow all the sauce to drip through.

10. Reduce to consistency and again with a ladle, gently pass through a sieve – do not force.

11. Finish with a splash of the sherry vinegar if needed and adjust seasoning.

12. Pass and chill.

Pheasant

4kg Chopped bones and trim
200g Shallots
200g Mushrooms
200g Carrots
2 tbsp Roasted flour
150g Sherry vinegar
½ Bottle Madeira
6kg Chicken stock
2 Sprigs thyme
1 Garlic bulb
1 Bay leaf
Redcurrant jelly, to taste

1. Cut the vegetables to a mirepoix.

2. Fry the trim in plenty of oil until well coloured. Add the vegetables, and colour.

3. Add the roasted flour and cook out for 2 minutes, stirring all the time. When all is golden brown, pass into a big colander and allow the oil to disperse.

4. Return the pan to the heat and deglaze with the sherry vinegar. Reduce by half.

5. Add the Madeira and reduce by half.

6. Return the meat and vegetables to the pan. Add the stock and the herbs and bring to the simmer and cook out for 2 hours – do not let it boil.

7. Mix in the redcurrant jelly and remove from the heat. Rest for 20 minutes.

8. With a ladle, gently pass through colander to a clean pan. Allow all the sauce to drip through.

9. Reduce to consistency and again with a ladle, gently pass through a sieve – do not force.

10. Finish with a splash of the sherry vinegar if needed and adjust seasoning.

11. Pass and chill.

Duck

4kg Trim
200g Shallots
200g Mushrooms
200g Carrots
150g Cabernet sauvignon
red wine vinegar
150g Red wine
150g Port
6kg Duck stock
2 Sprigs thyme
1 Garlic bulb
1 Bay leaf
Zest of 1 orange

1. Cut the vegetables to a mirepoix.

2. Fry the trim in plenty of oil until well coloured. Add the vegetables and when all is golden brown, pass into a big colander and allow the oil to disperse.

3. Return the pan to the heat and deglaze with the red wine vinegar. Reduce by half.

4. Add the red wine and reduce by half.

5. Add the port and reduce by half.

6. Return the meat and vegetables to the pan. Add the stock and herbs and bring to the simmer. Cook out for 2 hours – do not let it boil.

7. Remove from the heat and rest for 20 minutes.

8. With a ladle, gently pass through colander to a clean pan. Allow all the sauce to drip through.

9. Reduce to consistency and add the orange zest. Again with a ladle, gently pass through a sieve – do not force.

10. Finish with a splash of Forum if needed and adjust seasoning.

11. Pass and chill.

Chicken

2kg Chicken wings
200g Shallots
200g Mushrooms
200g Carrots
150g Sherry vinegar
150g White wine
150g Madeira
4kg Chicken stock
2 Sprigs thyme
1 Garlic bulb
1 Bay leaf
Salt and pepper, to taste

1. Cut the vegetables to a mirepoix.

2. Fry the trim in plenty of oil until well coloured. Though be careful; I take white meat to the colour of 'cornflakes', no further (any scorch will give a bitter taste to the sauce).

3. Add the vegetables, and colour. When all is golden brown, pass into a big colander and allow the oil to disperse.

4. Return the pan to the heat and deglaze with the sherry vinegar. Reduce by half.

5. Add the white wine and reduce by half.

6. Add the Madeira and reduce by half.

7. Return the meat and vegetables to the pan. Add the stock and the herbs and bring to the simmer. Cook out for 2 hours – do not let it boil.

8. Remove from the heat and rest for 20 minutes.

9. With a ladle, gently pass through colander to a clean pan. Allow all the sauce to drip through.

10. Reduce to consistency and add the orange zest. Again with a ladle, gently pass through a sieve – do not force.

11. Finish with a splash of sherry vinegar if needed and adjust seasoning.

12. Pass and chill.

Lamb & Balsamic

4kg Trim
200g Shallots
200g Mushrooms
200g Carrots
1 bottle White wine
6kg Lamb stock
2 Sprigs rosemary
1 Garlic bulb
1 Bay leaf
200g 8-Year Balsamic
vinegar

1. Cut the vegetables to a mirepoix.

2. Fry the trim in plenty of oil until well coloured, then add the vegetables. When all is golden brown, pass into a big colander and allow the oil to disperse.

3. Return the pan to the heat and deglaze with the white wine. Reduce by half.

4. Return the meat and vegetables to the pan. Add the stock and the herbs and bring to the simmer. Cook out for 2 hours – do not let it boil.

5. Remove from the heat and rest for 20 minutes.

6. With a ladle, gently pass through colander to a clean pan. Allow all the sauce to drip through.

7. Reduce to consistency and add the balsamic vinegar. Again with a ladle, gently pass through a sieve – do not force.

8. Adjust seasoning.

9. Pass and chill.

Venison & Chocolate

4kg Trim
200g Shallots
200g Mushrooms
200g Carrots
150g Cabernet sauvignon
red wine vinegar
150g Red wine
150g Port
6kg Venison shoulder liquid
150g Chocolate (70%)
2 Sprigs thyme
1 Garlic bulb
1 Bay leaf
Salt and pepper, to taste

1. Cut the vegetables to a mirepoix.

2. Fry the trim in plenty of oil until well coloured. Though be careful; I take white meat to the colour of 'cornflakes', no further (any scorch will give a bitter taste to the sauce).

3. Add the vegetables, and colour. When all is golden brown, pass into a big colander and allow the oil to disperse.

4. Return the pan to the heat and deglaze with the red wine vinegar. Reduce by half.

5. Add the red wine and reduce by half.

6. Add the port and reduce by half.

7. Return the meat and vegetables to the pan. Add the stock, herbs and chocolate and bring to the simmer. Cook out for 2 hours – do not let it boil.

8. Remove from the heat and rest for 20 minutes.

9. With a ladle, gently pass through colander to a clean pan. Allow all the sauce to drip through.

10. Reduce to consistency and add the orange zest. Again with a ladle, gently pass through a sieve – do not force.

11. Finish with a splash of Forum if needed and adjust seasoning.

12. Pass and chill.

Brine

Using a brine will help keep white lean meat particularly juicy during cooking. For pork and chicken, we use a 6% solution. i.e 6% salt to water.

1. Bring the water to the boil, add the salt and fully dissolve. Chill in the fridge. The brine must be fridge cold before adding any meat, so the best thing to do is make the brine a day or two before you need it. Thyme, bay and/or rosemary can be added too.

2. Four hours is a good rule of thumb for a chicken or pork loin.

Baked beetroot

This is not so much a recipe as a method. Depending on how many beets you have, season accordingly. We are eventually baking the beets in a marinade, so they should not be swimming in liquid.

Beetroots
Good lug of olive oil
Maldon sea salt
Thyme
Bay leaf
Good lug of red wine vinegar
1 Garlic clove, smashed

1. Pre-heat oven to 160°C.

2. Wash the beetroots then toss all of the ingredients together.

3. Wrap in a foil parcel and bake in oven. The beets are ready when a knife passes through with zero resistance.

4. Remove but allow to cool slightly in the foil.

5. Peel whilst they are still warm. The best method is to scrape with a small knife.

6. Chill until needed.

Baby onions

500g Baby onions
12g Salt
50g Butter
50g Water

1. Pre-heat the oven to 180°C.

2. Peel the skin from the onions.

3. In a heavy pan bring the water to the boil. Add the onions making sure that they are in a single layer. Place a lid on the pan and roast the onions in the oven until a sharp knife can be pushed through with no resistance.

4. Place on a tray in the fridge to cool.

Caramelised onions

We use these onions to mix though braised meat to balance out the richness.

Makes approximately 500g

10 Onions
100g butter
10g Roasted garlic pulp (see next page)
Salt and pepper, to taste

1. Peel the onions and slice them very finely.

2. In a heavy-based pan, add the butter, and over a high heat cook until it starts to turn a nutty brown. Add the garlic and the onions, but do not season them. Cook with a lid on, stirring every 2 or 3 minutes.

3. When the onions are very soft, remove the lid and continue to cook out any liquid that might be left. The onions are ready when they are golden brown and dry. At this point adjust the seasoning.

Roasted garlic pulp

500g Peeled garlic
250g Vegetable oil

1. Put the garlic and oil in a pan and cook in a very low oven (120°C) until the garlic is very soft, about 1 hour.

2. Transfer to a blender and blitz until smooth.

3. The pulp is now ready to be used as and when. As it is cooked it has a wonderful sweet nutty taste.

Cauliflower purée

1 Cauliflower
200g Whipping cream
Maldon sea salt
Truffle oil

1. Remove the core from the cauliflower and slice the florets as finely as possible.

2. Add the cauliflower and seasoning to a saucepan with the cream and cook out over a medium heat with a lid on until the cauliflower is very tender.

3. Blend the mix in a food processor until very smooth and add a few drops of truffle oil. Adjust the seasoning as required and pass through a fine sieve.

Jerusalem artichoke purée

500g Jerusalem artichokes
1 Garlic clove
120g Milk
Whipping cream, as required

1. Peel the artichokes and slice very thinly on a mandolin.

2. Add the artichoke slices and garlic to a pan and cover with milk. Bring to the simmer and cook out with a lid on. Transfer to a food processor and blend until smooth. If the mix is too dry add a little whipping cream as required.

3. Adjust the seasoning, then pass through a fine sieve into a clean pan.

Baby artichokes

Fresh artichokes are my favourite vegetable, they are easily ruined so care and love is needed – the end result is well worth it in my book.

20 Prepped baby artichokes
200g Olive oil
1 Carrot
2 Shallots
2 Garlic cloves
½ tsp Coriander seeds
½ tsp Fennel seeds
2 Star anise
50g White wine vinegar
100g White wine
Water
Maldon sea salt, to season

1. To 'turn' or prepare artichokes is a labour of love – and a real skill. With a small knife, remove the outer leaves, then gently peel away the tough outer skin. YouTube is probably the option here if you are not sure how to do it!

2. Toss the artichokes in the olive oil and a good dash of Maldon sea salt. Add to a hot pan and sweat off until well coated in the oil. Add the veg, garlic, seeds and star anise and sweat together until the vegetables have started to wilt and soften.

3. Add the vinegar and the wine and cook out for 2 minutes. Pour in the water until everything is just covered and bring to the boil.

4. Check seasoning. It needs to be fully seasoned at this stage – imagine you are tasting a soup. Cover with a paper cartouche and simmer – don't boil – for 10 minutes.

5. Once they're cooked through, allow to cool in the stock. They will not continue to cook so don't worry about them overcooking in the cool down process.

6. It's important to get the artichokes just right. Overcooked ones become mushy very quickly so if in doubt, keep checking them. Likewise, undercooked one aren't too pleasant either.

Mashed potatoes

In the restaurant we use four different types of mashed potatoes.

Dry mash

The base for the different types of mashed potatoes. Bake potatoes in the oven, scoop out the filling and pass through a potato mouli. You will have 70% of the original weight of potato that you started with. ie 1kg of potato will yield 700g of dry mash.

To spoon

Very soft and creamy.

170g Butter
100g Milk
70g Double cream
500g Dry mash (cooked in
the jackets)
Table salt

1. Melt the butter, milk and cream in a pan. Add the dry mash and whisk until smooth and hot. Season to taste.

To pipe

A little stiffer.

150g Butter
50g Milk
500g Dry mash
Table salt

1. Melt the butter and milk in a pan. Add the dry mash and whisk until smooth and hot. Season to taste.

To crisp

Gives a lovely crust when grilled or baked in the oven.

25g Butter
500g Dry mash
1 Egg yolk
4g Sea salt
4g White pepper

1. Melt the butter in a pan. Add the dry mash and whisk until smooth and hot.
2. Remove from the heat and beat in the egg yolk, salt and pepper.

Chargrilled potatoes

The best way to cook new potatoes, in my humble opinion, is in a steamer pan as they don't become wet and waterlogged. Use Kentish New or Jersey Royals for best results.

1. Cook a required amount of potatoes, and allow to cool. Cut into 5mm slices, discarding the first and last slice of each potato that is covered in skin.

2. Pre-heat a chargrill and grill the potatoes on one side only. Arrange the potatoes grill side up on a small tray and drizzle with olive oil and seasoning. They will absorb the oil as they rest in a warm place.

Potato cages

These can be made a few hours in advance.

2kg Water
80g Salt
2kg Maris Piper potatoes
200g Vegetable oil

1. Pre-heat the oven to 170°C.

2. Mix the water and the salt – it will taste quite salty!

3. Wash and peel the potatoes and using a 'turning slicer', cut the potato into 'spaghetti'. Pull off only the long strands and put them into the salt water. The salt will break the potato down and when the strands start to go floppy they are ready.

4. Wash the potatoes under fresh water, and then put in to a bowl with the vegetable oil.

5. Take six 6cm metal rings and rub them with oil. Wrap them in baking paper that has been cut to the same height as the rings. Now, find the start of a few of the potato strands and wrap the potato around the individual rings so that the rings have a uniform covering of potato all around them.

6. Place the potato rings in the oven and cook for 5 minutes to set the potato.

7. Remove from the oven and deep-fry at 170°C (still with the metal ring in place) until the potato is golden all over. Remove from the fryer, allow to cool for 5 minutes and then slide the ring from the potato.

Rice pudding

This is a delicious rice pudding in its own right, but is also the basic base that we use for our soufflés.

1kg Milk
700g (+300g) Double cream
Pinch of salt
6 Vanilla pods
240g Rice
180g Sugar

1. Pre-heat the oven to 120°C.

2. Bring the milk, 700g of double cream, salt, vanilla pods, rice and sugar to the simmer. Pop a lid on the pan and cook in the oven. When all of the liquid has been absorbed the pudding is ready to come out of the oven.

3. Add the extra 300g of cream and allow the rice to absorb it. Whilst still hot, blend the rice in a food processor and pass through a fine sieve. Chill until needed. The purée will keep in the fridge for three days.

Strawberry syrup

This is the most delicious strawberry syrup and is wonderful with champagne!

Makes approximately 700g

1kg Strawberries
150g Sugar
1 Bunch mint stalks
Lemon juice

1. Place all of the ingredients into a large bowl and cover tightly with clingfilm. Sit over a pan of gently simmering water for 2 hours. The strawberries will have released all of their natural juices. Add a few drops of lemon juice if needed.

2. Pass the juice through a large colander and then through a fine sieve. Chill until required.

Tuile baskets

The little crisp presentation baskets for ice creams and desserts.

100g Butter
200g Sifted icing sugar
210g Egg whites
200g Flour

1. Pre-heat the oven to 180°C.

2. Cream the butter and the icing sugar. Whisk in the egg whites and then beat in the flour.

3. We use a circular template cut from an ice cream container lid 7cm in diameter. Place the template on a silicone mat and spread the mix uniformly over the hole. Remove the template to leave a circle of tuile mix. Repeat to cover the mat.

4. Cook for approximately 5 minutes or until golden. Working very quickly, sandwich each tuile between two dariole moulds to form the basket shape. This is a tricky procedure and does take some practice.

White chocolate mousse

100g Milk
100g Double cream
20g Sugar
40g Egg yolks
300g White chocolate
225g Double cream

1. Bring the milk and cream to the boil. In a separate bowl whisk the sugar and the egg yolks. Beat the two together and cook out until the custard thickens and will coat the back of a spoon.

2. Remove from the heat, add the white chocolate and whisk for 2 more minutes. Pour the white chocolate custard through a fine sieve and allow to cool in a large bowl, but don't put it in the fridge.

3. When it has cooled to 20ºC, whisk the 225g of double cream to soft peaks and fold in the white chocolate custard. Refrigerate to set.

Custard & ice cream

Ice cream is essentially a custard base that has been freeze-churned. The method for the custard and most ice cream bases is the same.

CITRUS CUSTARD
Makes 1 litre of custard
For the sabayon:
8 Egg yolks
200g Sugar
8g Cornflour
Zest of 1 lemon
Juice of 2 lemons

For the liquid:
500g Milk
500g Cream

VANILLA ICE CREAM
Makes 1 litre of ice cream base
For the sabayon:
12 Egg yolks
130g Sugar

For the liquid:
500g Double cream
500g Milk
70g Sugar
4 Vanilla pods

1. In a kitchen mixer, whisk the sabayon ingredients until light and doubled in volume. Bring the liquid ingredients to the boil.

2. If you mix one straight into the other the egg yolks will curdle and the custard base will be grainy in texture, so we 'temper' the two together. Add one large ladle of the boiling liquid to the sabayon, and whisk the two together. Now tip the sabayon into the boiling liquid, whisking as you go. Continue to whisk until the custard has thickened and reaches 75ºC on a thermometer.

3. Remove from the heat and continue to whisk for at least 2 minutes. Cool the pan down in a sink filled with cold water, and whisk for 2 more minutes. Pass the custard base though a fine sieve and chill in the fridge. Only churn ice cream if the custard is fridge cold.

PRODUCT INFORMATION

ITEM *LAMB*

A-Z of Recipes

Produced by: